White Tara
HEALING LIGHT OF WISDOM

Ringu Tulku Rinpoche

with Mary Heneghan

BODHICHARYA PUBLICATIONS

Bodhicharya Publications is a Community Interest Company registered in the UK.
38 Moreland Avenue, Hereford, HR1 1BN, UK
www.bodhicharya.org Email: publications@bodhicharya.org

©Bodhicharya Publications 2022

Ringu Tulku asserts the moral right to be identified as the author of this work.
Please do not reproduce any part of this book without permission from the publisher.

ISBN 978-1-915725-00-4
First edition: 2022, Tibetan Year of the Water Tiger
Compiled and edited by Mary Heneghan

Teaching sources:

Shamatha, Vipassana and Mahamudra through Deity Yoga, using the White Tara sadhana as an example; Summer camp, Portugal, August 2017. Transcribed and edited by Mary Heneghan.

Teachings on the White Tara Sadhana; given by Ringu Tulku online, from Gangtok, Sikkim, 15th - 17th June 2020. Transcribed and edited by Mary Heneghan.

English translation of *Drolkar Gyünkhyer Düpa, A Short Daily practice for White Tara* by Tenga Rinpoche, based on a line-by-line translation and commentary by Ringu Tulku, 2020. Transcribed and edited by the Bodhicharya team, including Mary Heneghan, with advice from Adam Pearcey.

Instructions on the Six Protection Lights as part of White Tara practice; Ringu Tulku teaching at Bodhicharya Meditation Centre, Sikkim, India, March 2017. Notes taken by Mary Heneghan.

Typesetting and design by Paul O'Connor at Judo Design
Cover image: from a thangka painting of White Tara by R. D. Salga

"I want to share with you a feeling I have. I feel that my love does not have to remain within the limitations of my own life or body. I imagine that if I am no longer in the world, my love could still be present. I want to place my love on the moon and let the moon hold my love. Let the moon be the keeper of my love, offering it to everyone, just as the moon sends its light to embrace the whole earth."

His Holiness 17th Gyalwang Karmapa, Ogyen Trinley Dorje

Contents

Editor's Preface	viii
Introduction	1
Connecting skilful means with wisdom teachings	3
A healing practice	5
Motivation and practising Dharma	7
Learning another way of being	11
Visualisation practices	14
Questions and answers	20
White Tara Sadhana	27
Refuge	28
Compassion for ourselves and for others	34
Bodhicitta	36
Experiencing the pure being within us	41
A reminder of the ultimate nature of things	42
The visualisation	52

Two radiances	56
White Tara	59
Empowering the visualisation	65
Mantra recitation	70
Dissolution and Completion	78
Three Sacred Principles	82

Clarifying the Practice — 87
Further questions and answers — 91

Conclusion — 111
Healing — 111
Living and dying well — 114
The origin of Tara practice — 116

A Short Daily Practice for White Tara — 121

Six Protection Lights — 132

Glossary and Notes — 139

Acknowledgements — 150

ༀ་ཏུ་རེ་ཏུཏྟ་རེ་ཏུ་རེ་སྭཱ་ཧཱ།

Editor's Preface

This volume of Ringu Tulku's teachings on the practice of White Tara has been put together from two main teaching sources. Firstly, his teachings at summer camp in Portugal in August 2017 and secondly, his online teachings in June 2020 which were given from Gangtok, Sikkim, India. Further detail (particularly on the Six Protection Lights visualisation) was supplied by notes taken at retreat teachings in Sikkim in March 2017. And the English translation given of Tenga Rinpoche's sadhana of White Tara was put together from Ringu Tulku's line-by-line commentary on the text, recorded in 2020.

This book was many years in preparation, but the impetus to complete it came when sponsorship was kindly offered. This also meant that the finalised book can now, not only bring you Ringu Tulku's precious teachings on White Tara, but at the same time raise funds for Rigul Trust, a charity under the umbrella of Bodhicharya. The main aims of Rigul Trust are to offer the people of Ringu Tulku's homeland, in Rigul, Kham, access to sustained health care, poverty-relief and education. This is made possible through funding a health clinic, a school which provides hot meals for the children as well, and a shedra for monastic learning. Given the nature of Tara, perhaps this is particularly appropriate for this book.

I once asked Mindrolling Jetsün Khandro Rinpoche about the different qualities of the feminine deities represented in Tibetan Buddhism, particularly Vajrayogini, Tara and Yeshe Tsogyal. She explained: 'There is no distinction in the essential nature of all three. The very fundamental nature is Vajrayogini. Her manifest form is Tara. The expressivity of that nature is Yeshe Tsogyal. Vajrayogini is the essential nature, free from ego-grasping. Anything free from ego-grasping, that is the natural expressivity of your own nature, unimpededly arising - that can be called Tara. That then manifests in the form of your activities.' The teachings within this book, and the practice they describe, offer us a path towards genuinely realising, and actualising, what these pithy words mean.

We hope these teachings are of true benefit to you, the reader, and all those whose lives are touched by you. The practice of White Tara is so beautiful: in creating space and peace and healing, it puts us in touch with the wisdom light of life. This light is always shining in the midst of life but sometimes we cannot see it; sometimes our vision is clouded or we have forgotten about its possibilities. If something can help put us back in touch with that, on a daily basis, it could connect us to all we seek. The potential is always right here, right now; but we have to learn how to see it and how to develop it in our lives.

Following this wisdom light, through whatever we have to face, and for however long it takes, I think we cannot go wrong. So, in camaraderie and with the best of heart wishes, we offer you this volume of teachings. May it bring you joy, peace and well-being and give you a way to access all that may enlighten you.

Mary Dechen Jinpa
For Bodhicharya Publications

ༀ་ཏུ་རེ་ཏུཏྟ་རེ་ཏུ་རེ་སྭཱ་ཧཱ།

INTRODUCTION

Margaret Richardson, of Rigul Trust, requested me to teach on Tara and give an explanation of a short daily practice or sadhana of Tara. It is very common in many centres to practise Green Tara, with the Praises to 21 Taras, but then this can be quite a long practice. And I think this practice must have been taught many times in different centres by many great masters. So, I was looking for something very short and simple, yet precise, that we could go through. And I found this short sadhana composed by His Eminence Tenga Rinpoche, for the practice of White Tara, so this will be the focus of our study here.

Tenga Rinpoche was the Vajra Master of Rumtek Monastery, appointed by His Holiness 16th Karmapa, so in a way he was the Vajra Master of the whole of the Karma Kagyu lineage. And then, he was one of the greatest teachers I have ever seen. Many of those who met him would remember that he was just compassion, in person. He cannot be explained in any other way. I have often spoken about how, when I went to see him in Singapore where he was staying, after he had had both his legs amputated, I asked him how his health was. And he replied, 'Ah, everything is okay. Everything is completely without problem.' And he started to ask me about my health and whether I had any problems. So that, by the end of the meeting, it looked like I was the one who might need help with a problem, and he did not at all!

Then, when he came back to Nepal, I asked him for an empowerment, the empowerment of Vajrakilaya. In spite of all the problems he was facing, he made all the arrangements to do so, without hesitation. And he was always like that. When he passed away, he was sitting in meditation posture, in such a convincing state of *tukdam*, completely upright and without anything to lean on. So, he was really an accomplished and realised Bodhisattva, and I have no doubt whatsoever that any text composed by him holds a lot of blessing within it.

There are many different kinds of Tara practice: Green Tara, White Tara, Yellow Tara, Red Tara, 108 different Taras, 21 Taras, so many types of Tara practice. All of them are basically the same. Tara is one of the greatest Bodhisattvas, and one of the things about Tara is that she made a point, or a vow, that in all her lives as a Bodhisattva, she would always manifest as a female being. From the Buddhist point of view, male and female are just outer symbols. There is nothing male or female about the mind, it is the same in both male and female. You can manifest as a male; you can manifest as a female; it doesn't make any difference. But Tara made a point that she would always manifest in female form.

So, therefore, Tara is known as the Mother of all the Buddhas. Because of her association with the female form, she has this 'mother energy,' which is completely loving. Mothers are the bravest fighters for the protection of their children. Nobody can be more loving, or fiercer in their love, to protect others, than a mother for her children. So, Tara's blessing is always seen as very swift to respond and protect from all kinds of problems and sufferings, all kinds of outer, inner and negative dangers and pitfalls and attacks. This goes for all Tara practices.

Then, White Tara is regarded as especially powerful for healing. So, the practice we are going to look at here can be regarded as especially powerful to generate healing power, to give long life and to eliminate diseases and all kinds of problems and suffering. Its main benefits are usually said to be for long life, increasing positive energy, increasing wisdom and increasing all the positive aspects of ourselves.

Furthermore, White Tara practice is regarded as very auspicious, which can be seen by the many great masters of the past who have used White Tara as their main practice or their *yidam*. The 16th Karmapa, Jamgong Kongtrul the Great, Jamyang Khyentse Wangpo, Atisha Dipamkara, and many other great masters, all used White Tara as their main *yidam* practice.

Connecting skilful means with wisdom teachings

Generally, in Buddhism, we talk about wisdom and method: profound wisdom and skilful means. And it is often said that both are equally important. They say these two aspects of the teachings are like two wings of a bird. If one wing is not strong, it is not possible to fly. So, therefore, there are many teachings given on both aspects. Wisdom teachings are concerned with meditation and view and include all the various teachings on Mahamudra and Ngöndro. Mahamudra teachings are considered to be the most profound and the deepest teachings of the Kagyu lineage, and I think they are helpful, and useful, for us. Even if we don't really have the most profound understanding and experience, I think even a small amount of understanding and practice helps in our lives.

As well as the wisdom teachings, many practices are given which pertain to the skilful means side, especially in Vajrayana Buddhism. The sadhana we are going to look at here would be an example of these. But it seems to me that sometimes people have particular difficulties when we talk about and try to practise these kinds of teachings. Maybe this happens because it is not explained clearly enough. Or it could be that these practices seem to be too much coloured by tradition or culture. Sometimes I feel that, with these kinds of Vajrayana practices, people cannot see how they actually contain those very wisdom teachings that we have been talking about, Mahamudra and so forth; they cannot see the connection.

It is very important to connect these two things: the skilful means, for example Vajrayana practices, and the wisdom teachings. Then these methods become something we can use to work on ourselves. Most of these practices, whether we are talking about certain kinds of visualisations or whatever, are not only a tradition, they are not only linked with a certain time or culture. They are actually a training, a skilful way to work on our habitual tendencies. Essentially, they are the same as any other type of meditation; they are just different ways of doing the same mindful meditation. But they introduce a little more than just a simple focus for the mind. In order to really work on our negative habits, emotions, and addictions, they give us a little bit of something more to work on them with.

Therefore, the focus of these teachings on the practice of White Tara will be to look at the sadhana of White Tara, a simple kind of Vajrayana practice, which is a special kind of a healing practice. And as we look at it, we will also focus on finding these wisdom teachings we are talking about within it – namely meditation, including different levels of meditation, like *shamatha* meditation, *vipassana* meditation, Mahamudra and so forth. We will look at how these are all contained within this practice, as well as all the other ways of working on ourselves. This is the essence of what it is all about. Vajrayana practices are about the whole of practice, not just one area or one side. They are a holistic practice, including everything.

A healing practice

We have mentioned how White Tara is a powerful healing practice. I think healing practices are very necessary at this moment in time, for everybody. We all need healing, personally in our lives, but we also need healing for the world and for society in general. We need healing for everything. There are lots of negative things happening, there is a lot of fear and a lot of anger, and I think many people are focussing on these negative things. This is nothing new, of course, but if more and more people focus on negative things, that will not only make the whole world seem more hopeless and more negative for us, but also brings us a negative outlook for our own life.

How we feel, and how we are, are very much dependent on how we focus our mind. If I am only ever focussing on negative things, negative happenings in my life or around the world, then my mind will become negative, because that is what I am focussing my mind on. It can become such that there is nothing good, nothing positive, for me anymore; everything becomes negative and bad. There is nothing to rejoice about, nothing to be happy about, nothing to learn from. It is very sad and bleak and joyless.

But if we focus our mind on more positive things, whether it is in our life, in our mind, in our emotions, or around the world, there are still lots of positive things happening. Then we have hope; we become encouraged and inspired, courageous, positive and joyful, and more determined. And that is what we really need. It is very important. This is what we need to train on, I think, because it is very easy to focus on negative things. Which means it is very easy to become angry; it is very easy to complain; it is very easy to become pessimistic; it is very easy to be overtaken by fear, anxiety and all those kinds of things. What these teachings are about, is not allowing that to happen.

Instead, we focus our mind on healing: healing ourselves, healing everybody, healing the whole world - and not only the whole world, but the whole cosmos! I am not suggesting this will happen immediately, that after doing some practice you will go out into the world and find everything is healed. But it is true that how you see the world is dependent on your mood, on your own state of mind. If you are in a good mood, everything seems brighter – you notice the flowers, people seem friendlier, everybody smiles at you, you feel so much at ease you don't even realise that you are smiling at them. So, therefore, how the world is, is a lot to do with how you are. I think it is very important to understand this. My father used to say, 'If you are not bad, nobody will be bad to you.' He really believed this, and I think there is some wisdom in it.

Motivation and practising Dharma

In this field, which is sometimes called Buddhism, we find many teachings that were not actually directly taught by Buddha Shakyamuni. In a strict sense, you cannot say they are part of Buddhism because they do not come directly from Buddha Shakyamuni, but they are a part of Dharma. So, therefore, 'Buddhism' is not really a correct term to use. It is more correct to talk about 'Dharma' and practising Dharma. Buddha talked about Dharma practice. Buddha never used a word like Buddhism and Buddha never said that his teaching was the only Dharma teaching. Buddha said that there have been many, many Buddhas before him, and there will be many, many Buddhas after him, and *all* their teachings will be on Dharma. Therefore, the importance is not given to Buddhism but to Dharma.

If somebody is living his or her life according to the Dharma then, even if that person had never heard about the Buddha, he or she is practising the Dharma. And also, if somebody is doing something which is good for themselves and good for others, which is helping them transform and develop their positive side, even if that is not directly taught by Buddha, that is also Dharma.

Then, a fundamental teaching, which is universally accepted, at least in Tibet, is that you may practise Dharma for different reasons. I think this is also very important. Atisha Dipamkara, one of the main teachers of Dharma, who came from India to Tibet, explained this in his teachings. He taught all the mind-training teachings, which are the basis of the *Lam Rim*, or Graded Path, teachings. This is the most common and accepted path among all the various schools of Tibetan Buddhism.

Atisha's most important, classic text is called *The Lamp for the Path to Enlightenment* and in that he says that, because there are many different types of people and because they all need different teachings and different ways to follow, so Buddha taught many different ways. But then, he said that he could more or less categorise all these different types of people who practised Dharma into three types. And this is a very common way of speaking about this, in all the Graded Path or mind-training teachings, in the common teachings in Tibet. We talk about three different types of people:

The first includes those people who wish to practise Dharma in order to have a happy life in the world, just a happy samsaric life. They are not concerned with enlightenment. Many people don't know what enlightenment is, and don't care about it either. They just want to have a nice, happy, samsaric life. And, for that, you can practise Dharma. And that is very good. That is possible and that is very good. That is part of what the teachings are taught for. This is category one. It is not about short-term enjoyment and then getting into trouble later. It is not just about having a party or a picnic. It is a little bit long-term, taking the whole of life into account.

Then there is another type of person, who it is possible may have tried the method above, to have a happy meaningful life. But then they slowly found out that to really have a completely happy life, you need to learn, not only how to live, but also how to die, properly. And then, in order to do that, one needs to learn deeply how to face anything that happens - because all different kinds of things can happen. And then, in order to work on that, you find you need to work deeply on your emotions and your habitual tendencies, in order to transform your way of seeing and your way of experiencing.

Then these people understand that there is something a little bit deeper than just having a nice life in this life, or in the next life. They start to understand that there is something a little bit more. They start to appreciate the possibility of what we call *nirvana* or enlightenment. So, then these people start to practise Dharma for that end, to really transform themselves completely. This is the second category or reason people may practise Dharma. It is not that they are only trying to attain enlightenment, and are not concerned about anything good in this life. These two things can go together. If you are really working for enlightenment, you are becoming a better human being and therefore you are also preparing to live a happier, more purposeful, good life. Both go together, it is not like you have to choose one or the other.

Then there are other people who are not only concerned about their own liberation or freedom or enlightenment. They are not concerned about a better life or a happier life for themselves only. They are concerned about other people as well. They are concerned about their own near and dear ones, but they are also concerned about the near and dear ones of *those* people, and *their* near and dear ones, and *their* near and dear ones, and so eventually, everybody. And they are concerned, not just for a better life for now, but for lasting happiness, and for all the beings.

This is what we call a Bodhisattva type of person, or altruistic type of person. People who are compassionate and courageous, people who are not satisfied and content with just having a happier and better life for themselves. They are not content and satisfied with their own freedom from suffering and finding *nirvana* or enlightenment. They really feel that, unless other people can also be free from suffering, then it is not worth it. So, therefore, they practise Dharma not only for themselves, but for everybody. And these people are called Bodhisattvas.

Generally speaking, there are these three kinds of categories of people who practise Dharma. And of course, if you are practising Dharma in order to benefit everybody else, that does not mean that you yourself cannot be liberated, cannot become enlightened. Because if, in order to help everybody, you work towards becoming more compassionate and wiser, then you naturally become not only happier and have a more meaningful life, but you will also become very much transformed in the process, and may even attain enlightenment – whether you like it or not!

These are the three different types of people described. It is sometimes called three different paths but actually it is not really three different paths, it is three different *purposes* for the practise of Dharma. When we talk about Dharma practice, we need to consider all these different types of people. There are many teachings and books in Dharma that presuppose the reader is the last type of person. But it is not totally correct to only talk about that type of person. Maybe that is not your purpose.

What kind of purpose I have, for whatever I do, including learning the Dharma, that is something that I have to decide for myself. I have to have my own reasons why I practise Dharma. That would be informed by whatever you learn from teachings, from retreats, from whatever you engage with. This is a basic tenet. If there is a book and it is written from the point of view of the Bodhisattva path, then it may say, 'I practise Dharma for the sake of all beings…' It may be written like that for that point of view, but it does not mean that you have to take that on.

Sometimes people ask, 'The teachers say I should practise Dharma in order to become enlightened, but I don't really care about enlightenment, because I don't really know what enlightenment is. There may be nothing called enlightenment, so why do I have to do this?' So, I think it is very important to be clear that Dharma can be practised for enlightenment, but also for a nice life, a good life. And, of course, you can practise for all the sentient beings as well, if you want to.

Learning another way of being

Sometimes it seems that to practise for enlightenment should be very easy – people say you just have to recognise your own true nature. In one way, that is true. From the Buddhist point of view, enlightenment is not something *out there*, that you have to cross seven oceans and then do all kinds of tests for, in order to finally find it somewhere in a secret cave. It is not like that. It is just recognising ourselves, and our own potentials. But, because we are so strongly habituated – or maybe I should say addicted – to a way of looking at things, and reacting as we do now, it is very difficult to change this. That is why most of the practice is about this, changing our habits, our habitual tendencies. If we are used to seeing things in a certain way, or doing things in a certain way, we sometimes can't even imagine that there could be another way of seeing things or doing things differently.

In India, the way we eat food is very habitual. I don't know if this is of interest to you, but it was quite interesting to me: I found out that there is a clear, vertical line through the map of India, which goes through the middle of Bihar. And, exactly described by this line, everybody to the east of this line eats rice and everybody to the west of this line eats wheat. East of that line, they think rice is the only staple food. So that, when they want to ask if someone has eaten food, they ask if they have eaten rice. To the west of that line, to ask if someone has eaten food, you ask if they have eaten *roti* [flat bread]. It is that delineated.

I come from the rice-eating side of the line, which includes Nepal, Sikkim, Bhutan, Bengal. And then, from there onwards – Burma, Thailand, China, everywhere up to Japan - they all eat rice. In some places the rice should be sticky; in some places every grain must be separate; in some places rice must be served very hot; in other places the rice must be cold before they will serve it. In all these places, we expect lots of rice, and a little bit of vegetable or something to go with it. Then when we come to the West, they only serve a little bit of rice on the side. I have known people feel like they never get a proper meal, because they don't get the food they are used to.

We are so habituated to a certain way of eating, or of doing anything. We cannot imagine there is another way of doing things. It is very difficult then for us to change. There are many ways in which we react, or see things, that cause us so many problems – problems for ourselves and also for others – but somehow we still think it is the only way we can react. It is very difficult for us to even understand this problem that we have. To change or correct it, by doing something different, is therefore even more difficult.

We all experience anger; we all experience worry; we all experience stress. We all have little problems that we can't help holding onto, that we cannot let go of. We feel that it is not possible to do otherwise. We cannot imagine not feeling bad if somebody does something to us. Or we feel that it is impossible to be free from anxiety and fear and worries. We assume it is impossible not to get upset and angry if somebody does something we don't like. So, therefore, we react in these ways and we have lots of pain; we have many problems. We don't know there is another way of being, another way of thinking, another way of seeing.

Many of the teachings in Dharma are about this. In many ways, they are very simple, but sometimes the simplest things are the most difficult to actualise. For example, it is true that meditation is often not easy for many people. But I think most of the time the reason meditation is not easy, is not because it is not easy in itself, but simply because people don't know how to do it. A teacher can tell you a hundred times about meditation but that does not necessarily help you. Because learning something that is practical is something that cannot really be taught at all. I learned this very clearly myself when I learnt to drive a car - I did not really learn to drive a car very well, but I learned so many other things from the process!

I learnt that one cannot really teach such a thing, a practical thing. I had more than ten teachers, all of them very good; one of them was actually training pilots to fly planes. Of course, his instructions were very good. He said, 'When you are driving you have to be aware of everything, of all the ten directions,' and so forth. Theoretically, it is very nice to hear how to do everything, but practically I had to learn for myself. His telling me to be aware is not what makes me aware. That is something I have to do myself. And there are lots of examples like this.

Of course, driving a car is essentially very simple. There is a steering wheel, and a brake and an accelerator, and then changing the gear. But knowing how to do it does not mean that you *can* do it, when you come to do it. You know what you *should* do, but you do not *do* it - and sometimes you even do the opposite! Instead of stopping, you accelerate. You know it is wrong, but you still do it. This kind of learning is all about doing. You have to do it and do it and do it. And yet, you may feel you are not learning anything at all and get upset with yourself, 'Why am I still doing it like this?!' Whether you can really learn something varies from person to person. It needs a lot of training and exercising and practice, in order that you might become able to do it.

Intellectual understanding is important, but understanding alone is not enough. The major part is practising. And it is exactly like this with Dharma. Practising Dharma is actually living. Sometimes people don't understand this and think the only important thing is the understanding. They gain some understanding and then wonder why it has not changed them. It is because practising and understanding are two different things.

Usually, of course, we start with understanding but then it has to be supported by practice. We need to use our understanding again and again in our life. This is why we put a strong emphasis on meditation in the Dharma. We talk about all different kinds of meditation, because they are our means of familiarising ourselves with what we have understood.

Visualisation practices

The traditional way to learn a practice like this one would usually be that Tibetan lamas would come and give what is called an empowerment. Then they would instruct the students to practise that particular *sadhana*, perhaps calling it a *yidam*. That would be the traditional Tibetan way. It is true that these are very profound teachings, given in this way, but this is very different from the Western way of doing things.

For example, these are visualisation practices, but many people say, 'I cannot visualise.' But actually, everybody visualises. Maybe it is the word 'visualisation' which is not correct. I sometimes ask the question, 'Where are you going on holiday next?' Maybe someone says, 'Oh, we are going to Portugal...or Spain... or the Bahamas...' And I say, 'What are you going to do there?' 'Oh, we are going to lie down on the beach. We are going to sunbathe and walk on the beach, with the lovely sand and everything...' I ask, 'Can you think about that? Can you picture it? Can you imagine it?' 'Oh, yes!' *That is* visualisation.

You can think about a nice visualisation like this, but all the bad things we can think about are also visualisation: 'This can go wrong... That can go wrong...' We could think about those, and it may be very real, and very clear, to us. That is visualisation, too. Because visualisation is just living through a certain thing that is not here now. Putting our mind in a certain situation, bringing something into our mind.

We could think about something very nice from the past. I think all of us must have had some very nice experience from the past, perhaps from childhood, some very happy, joyful experience. If we go back to that experience, and close our eyes and try to be in that situation, and feel we are living through that experience, what happens? We feel very nice. I'm sure you could see a smile on my face if I were doing that.

It is the same thing with a very bad situation, a terrible or unhappy situation. If I go back and visualise that, and live through that again, that is also visualisation. I could feel very unhappy, or sad, or angry. So, what do we usually do? Usually, are we thinking about bad things from the past or the future? Or good things from the past or the future?

Actually, this is what decides what kind of a person we are. The more we think about bad things, the more bad things fill our mind, and we dwell on them, the more we are an unhappy person. And the more we dwell on good things, the more we are a happy person. I think this is mostly how it works. If I am more aware of, and remember more, positive things, good things, nice things, that I experience now or that I experienced before, I become happy. That habit makes me a happier person. But if I think more about something difficult and problematic, hurtful and unhappy, the more it is in my mind, the more I become unhappy and even depressed.

How important is it to remember all those bad things? How crucial is it? How important is it for us to think about all the bad things that have happened to us? So that we have to think about them again and again, and again and again, *and again and again...* In what way does this help us? It only makes us unhappy. It is not that by thinking about it, we can change the past. It doesn't really bring much good at all. So then why do we do it? Many people have this habit of remembering every small bad thing that happened, but forgetting all the good things that have happened. If we could change this a little bit, then we could be living a much happier life.

So, what can we do to change this? The only thing I can do is to train myself to focus on positive things, from now on. There are always lots of positive, and lots of less positive things, going on. What comes to my mind most easily? Which do I see first? Usually, most of the time, we tend to look for the bad things. It is a habit we have. It helps to focus our mind on something positive, and make that a habit.

Again and again, think about something positive. It is not that you have to forget the bad things, although sometimes you can forget them. It is more that lots of things happen in life. Lots of people say lots of things, some very nice things, some not so nice things, and then we have a choice about what we remember. We can try to remember the nice things and not worry too much about the less nice things.

Somebody gave me very good advice once. You know when you have that kind of person, sometimes even in your own family, who is always complaining and saying not so nice things. You cannot deny it is happening, maybe it is an old person who has become like this, or whatever. But the advice I received was just to let it come in one ear and go out the other one. As they are talking, you just say, 'Ah yes, yes, yes...' but it is straight out of your head immediately. And actually, this is very helpful. Because sometimes, before I have even forgotten what they said, they have forgotten it themselves; especially if it is an old person. So, why should I keep hold of it? Sometimes, something someone says, people keep hold of it for *so* long. The Vajrayana training of visualisation is exactly to work with this kind of thing.

When we meditate, there are different ways of meditating. Sometimes we meditate without an object of meditation. We let our mind rest; not in the past, not too much in the future, but just *being*. We are a little bit aware of what is going on and then we just relax in that. Whatever is happening, we just let it pass on, and pass on, and pass on... If you hear something, you hear it. If you see something, you see it. You don't need to especially focus your mind on anything in particular. But sometimes this way of meditating is a little bit difficult. In the beginning, it is usually too difficult to just do this. So then, you need something to focus on, to bring your mind back if you are distracted.

Therefore, we can use an object to focus our mind on. For example, sometimes we use our breathing for this. Breathing is a very good thing to use, unless you have a breathing problem. If you have a breathing problem, it may not work so well to focus on it, but otherwise it can be very helpful. We have to breathe anyway, so we just remain a little bit aware of our breathing. Of course, we cannot stop whatever happens in our mind, but we don't have to stop it all, we just remain a little bit aware of our breathing as everything else comes and goes.

Sometimes we may use an object that we can see, or hear, or we could use anything. For example, sometimes music is good. All these things are neutral things, neither good nor bad. For example, breathing is just there. But in the Vajrayana visualisation practices, we are using, as our focus, an embodiment of all good qualities - somebody who is very kind and compassionate, somebody who is like our very best friend, who only has good wishes for us, who is always wishing well to everybody, somebody who is full of compassionate wisdom. So, what are we doing then? We are using a focus for our mind, which is not only like an anchor to bring our mind back to if we are distracted, but the focus is also something positive and beneficial. It is not just a neutral focus; it includes the very qualities we want to train our mind to focus on. As we focus on this, our mind is occupied by these qualities, and we are feeling that energy.

In this way, we are meditating, but also cultivating our positive experience at the same time. We are using the same basic meditation technique, allowing our mind to lightly focus on something. Then, at the same time, we are also indirectly training our compassion. Because we feel somebody to be there who is an embodiment of great compassion, present with us. That is the practice of visualisation we use in a sadhana.

When we meditate – calm abiding or *shamatha* meditation - we are not always stuck in one thing, only one thing going on in our mind the whole time. If we see, we see. If we hear, we hear. If we smell, we smell. If we feel, we feel. If we have a thought, we have a thought. That can still be part of the meditation. But then, if we think, 'Oh, I have become distracted because I saw this, or heard this, or smelt this or felt this, or had this thought...' if we start thinking like this, then we have become distracted. Whether it is distraction or not depends on how we are with it. Seeing, hearing, thinking and so on, can be a distraction. Or they can be a continuation of your mindfulness.

If you hear something and you start thinking about it: 'Oh, I have heard these people; why are people not quiet while I am meditating; now I cannot meditate because of this noise...' and so on, then you are distracted. But if you hear something and you are aware of hearing it, you are just aware, and you are aware of your awareness. Now you are aware of seeing; now aware of a thought; now aware of an emotion... if you are aware like that, and mindful of that awareness, then there is no distraction, because you are continuously aware. When you are continuously aware, then you are not distracted.

In fact, sometimes when you are engaged in a visualisation, it is good to change your focus within that visualisation as well. This helps to keep you focused on the visualisation; it keeps you fresh and awake in meditation, so you don't become bored.

Questions and answers

Remembering the past

Student: If we don't look back on our past experiences, is there not a risk that we miss out on learning from our mistakes?

Rinpoche: Yes, it is maybe not even possible, not to remember the past. It is sometimes important to reflect on our past and it is good to reflect, and I think it is important to learn from the past – bad things and good things, also. Sometimes we learn from bad things, but we also learn from good things. But there is a classic saying, which I find to be a little bit correct: in this world, there is one thing about history which is true, and that is that nobody learns from history. We have so much history, and so much difficult history, and we know about it all; but it seems that history keeps repeating itself, nevertheless. We should have learnt from history, but it is very seldom that we do. I don't know why we don't learn from history, maybe we don't reflect enough, maybe we just follow our habits and so the same thing happens again and again.

Sometimes though, we learn from good things too. We can learn more from appreciation than from punishment. If somebody encourages us, even if we didn't do such a great thing but somebody says, 'Oh, you did really well...' Then we might find we can do even better next time. I think it is important to learn from appreciation – good things that have happened to me; good things that I have done; if I have done this well, then maybe I can do even better next time.

Visualisation / arising

Student: You were wondering if *visualisation* is the best word to use, would imagination be a better word? Because it includes all the senses, whereas visualisation tends to be about the visual side / seeing only.

Rinpoche: Yes, maybe misunderstanding starts because of the word not being quite right. In Tibetan the word used doesn't mean 'to see.' It means 'arising,' so it is about all the senses, our whole experience. Maybe imagination is a better word, but there is still the sense of 'image,' which is also about seeing.

Another point is that there are different kinds of people. Some are more visual, some are more focused on sound, and some are more focused mentally, on ideas and words. Accordingly, whichever modality is strongest for you, you should work with that first. For example, we use mantras for the sound aspect, sounds like *OM*. Then some people have more sense of feeling, and so they can focus more on the feeling than on the image. And then sometimes you can use all three - seeing, hearing and feeling - together.

Tibetan iconography

Student: Coming back to your analogy of visualising our holiday, what I have a problem with is visualising the Tibetan iconography, which doesn't feel very relevant to me or my life.

Rinpoche: This is something which I need to talk about. When Guru Padmasambhava was invited to Tibet and they were building the great monastery of Samye, they needed to construct many statues and this question arose then:

What image should they make the statues in? They discussed this at length. Some said that because Buddhism and Buddhist teachings came from India, the statues should be in the image of Indians. And some said that they should be in the image of the Nepalese, because the artists were mainly Nepalese. Then some said they should be in the image of Tibetans because the Tibetans could not imagine the other people very easily and wanted them to be in the image of Tibetans.

In the end, Guru Rinpoche accepted this last argument and said they should be made in the image of Tibetans. And actually, there are even names of people, in whose images the statues were made. For example, Tara was made in the image of one of the queens of the time, a very beautiful queen. We could actually find out the personal names of the people these first statues in Tibet were made of.

What all this suggests is that it is not necessary for Westerners to make the images in a Tibetan style, not at all. You can make your image look like a Westerner, a very beautiful or inspiring person, however works best for you. All the aspects like the dress and colours of the images, you can imagine these as you like, because the images we see on the thangkas are not necessarily how they *are*; they are the artist's image.

Healing or enlightenment?

Student: You said White Tara practice is good for healing, but can one think of it more as a training towards enlightenment, instead?

Rinpoche: Yes, of course, because basically any Dharma practice, whatever kind of practice it is, is about bringing out wisdom and compassion. And enlightenment is actually nothing else, other than developing your wisdom and compassion to their fullest. Tara practice is also for this, to develop wisdom and compassion. And then, why do we practise healing? That is also for this, for wisdom and compassion.

You could say, therefore, that we practise for many reasons. A bit like 'buy one, get two' – but more like 'buy one, get five!' We practise to work on our compassion, for enlightenment, for our own healing, for others' healing, to change our habits, to make ourselves happier, all these many different things. That is what we should try to do, something that will help us at every level. Good for me, good for others, good for now, good for the long run. Then it is very good.

Working on afflictive emotions

Student: How does this practice work on our afflictive emotions?

Rinpoche: Actually, the main thing is not the practice, but yourself. These practices are a method or a means, and that method, we need to apply it on ourselves. Now, if I can apply it, it will help. If I cannot, or do not, apply it, then it would not help. So, for instance, if we want to work on our negative emotions, we could categorise them into four or five basic types.

The first group of emotions could be anger, hatred and ill-will kind of emotions. When you have these emotions, you feel very disturbed; it is not good for you and it is not good for others, also. Therefore, they are regarded as negative. Then, another group of emotions is when there is too much greed, selfishness, attachment, clinging and miserliness. This group is also regarded as negative because these strong emotions make you always dissatisfied, so they bring unhappiness. Then there is jealousy and envy, which is about not being happy when somebody else has something very good. That is regarded as a negative emotion because it brings you unhappiness for no reason.

Then there could also be too much arrogance or too much pride; you can't see any good thing in anybody else because you are too much puffed up with your own pride. If you are like that, you can't learn anything because you can't see anything good outside of you. So that is also regarded as a negative emotion. And then there is the state of mind, which is maybe not an emotion, that is unclear or ignorant; you misunderstand things, you cannot see them clearly. That is also not a very good state of mind.

From the Buddhist point of view, these five groups are what we call mind poisons. They are not good for us. They bring problems, pain and suffering to ourselves and also to others. Now, how do we work on these? We need to reduce these five and increase the opposite of them. What is the opposite of all these? The opposite of ignorance and lack of clarity and misunderstanding is wisdom. Wisdom is when you see clearly, when you know fully, when your mind is clear and bright; that is wisdom. So, this is one thing that we need to increase.

Then, the opposite of the other four types of emotions is actually compassion. Compassion is good will, kindness, love; that is what we mean by compassion. When you are angry or upset or hateful, it is obvious to us that the opposite would be compassion. But also, if you are too greedy or clinging too much, the opposite is compassion. Because greed is 'I want, I want,' but compassion is 'I want to share, I want to give to others.' Greed and clinging are about tightening up towards myself, whereas compassion is opening out. Jealousy and envy are about not being happy that someone is getting something nice, whereas compassion is being happy about that, because I wish well towards everybody. And arrogance is too much about myself, a kind of megalomania, whereas compassion is altruistic, so it is the opposite.

So, if we can increase our compassion and wisdom, then we are working on all our negative emotions. When we are doing practice, for instance, one way of increasing our compassion is to think about somebody who is suffering, who has pain and problems, and then think to ourselves, 'Ah, this person has pain and problems; I really wish to help.' That is one way of working on compassion. Another way is to allow my mind to experience somebody who has complete loving-kindness and compassion. Here, you don't have to concentrate on the suffering of others. You can just go directly to the kindness, compassion, and love. By doing a practice like this Tara practice you are training directly, in that way. You are not concentrating on suffering. You are concentrating on your love, your compassion, your kindness, and trying to feel that.

So, here the technique is that we try to feel the positive aspect, directly. It does not mean that we don't have to use other ways of training also. For example, if I feel negative emotions or I have a negative reaction to something, then I have to say, 'Okay, this is a negative reaction; it's not very good for me and it's not very good for others. Maybe it is better that I let it go.' If I can let it go, I feel good. But sometimes, it happens that I cannot let it go. I react badly. I am angry. Then, I don't have to say, 'Oh I am angry, I am so bad, aaargh!' You don't have to beat yourself up about it. You realise, 'This is what I have been doing all my lives up till now. I have been angry all the time. I have been hateful all the time. I have been greedy all the time. I have been jealous all the time. It's nothing new. It's not that great, but it's nothing new. The sky is not going to fall on me. It's not very good but it's okay. I will slowly try to get it better.' That is the idea. There is no point hating yourself if you are a little bit not compassionate!

WHITE TARA SADHANA

There is a recording of Tenga Rinpoche chanting this White Tara sadhana that he composed, and even myself, I recorded myself singing it. I thought it might be helpful. But actually, neither of these sound great, especially the one I did!

When we practise sadhanas, there is often the issue of whether to practise in English or in Tibetan, or in both languages together. Different groups find different solutions. If you know the Tibetan, and you have a good voice, it is very nice to sing it in Tibetan. Because how it is written in Tibetan is very poetic and with a certain kind of a flow. But some people's chanting may not be up to that. So, in that case, you could say it in Tibetan.

Then, sometimes, people ask me if they can say the practice in English, because they don't understand the Tibetan. You can do that, of course. But then some of those same people came to me after some time and said they had been doing the practice in English, but it was not at all inspiring like that. So, then they decided to chant in Tibetan and say it through in English afterwards. But then, after some time, they found this did not work either because stopping to read the English broke up the flow of the practice.

There is no easy solution. The translation from Tibetan is not perfect, so far, neither in English nor in any other language. So, I think you have to find your own way with this. The important thing is the meaning, so you can do it in whatever way is best for this. It helps that this is a very short sadhana we are doing here. I did read somewhere that singing is very good for your mind. They say, if you sing a lot, your mind becomes much more positive, purer. It is even said to cure depression. So, if you can sing it, then maybe you should sing - from your heart!

[see Editor's Note in Glossary]

Refuge

Like any sadhana, this one starts with Refuge and Bodhicitta. The first two lines are the Refuge:

> Namo,
> sang gyä chö dang gen dün la
> go sum gü pay kyab su chi
>
> *Namo,*
> *With deep reverence and humility of body, speech and mind,*
> *I take refuge in Buddha, Dharma and Sangha.*

In Buddhism, we don't have a Creator God, but we have Buddhas and Bodhisattvas: many positive beings. People sometimes ask, 'You Buddhists don't have a God, so who do you pray to?' But in Buddhism, *who to pray to* is not seen as important as *what to pray for*.

The general understanding and belief from the Buddhist point of view is that I have the potential and the capacity to develop my positive qualities, like compassion and so forth; they can be awakened and cultivated in me. Scientists even confirm we usually only use a small proportion of the capacity of our mind.

Once we understand that it is possible for us to become transformed by developing our capacities and potentials, then it does not seem so unlikely that there could be beings who have achieved this in the past. And these beings are called Buddhas of the past, or Bodhisattvas if they are on the path. Those beings should be able to help us, because they have developed their compassion. If somebody is developing their compassion, what is the use, if they don't want to help anybody? And then if they have wisdom too, they must know how to help us. So, therefore, we pray to them, all the great beings. We ask for their help.

But, when we talk about taking refuge in Buddha – this I need to say again and again, because it is very often misunderstood – it is not about asking Buddha to save us, thinking that Buddha will just come and help us and that is all that is needed. It is not that Buddhas do not have the capacity to help, but going for refuge to the Buddha does not have that meaning. It is about Buddha within me. It is that I have the possibility to bring out my Buddha potential, to awaken the positive qualities within me, *like* the Buddhas of the past, Buddha Shakyamuni and all other enlightened beings.

It is my decision that I want to do that. I want to bring out my positive qualities, and awaken them, and I would like to do that for myself and also for other people.

Because, if I could do that, I would be able to help other people much more strongly and much more deeply. So, I would like to work towards that. That decision, that determination, is going for refuge to the Buddha.

Of course, by going for refuge to the Buddha, I take the enlightened beings of the past as my example. I follow their example. I receive their instructions, teachings and guidance, and I try to follow their footsteps. That is part of going for refuge to the Buddha, but basically it is my own decision to follow a certain path.

We have three refuges: Buddha, Dharma and Sangha. If it was only about Buddha coming and saving us, then we would not need the other two refuges, Dharma and Sangha. But, because it is not just about Buddha coming and saving me, it is something I have to do. This is sometimes the most difficult aspect of Buddhism, or Dharma.

I once asked some long-term Dharma students three questions; and I have never forgotten the answers one person gave. What I asked the students was: 'You have been studying Dharma for a long time now, practising and so forth; but, in all your experience of Dharma, what is the worst thing for you, what do you dislike the most about Dharma? And what is it that you like the most, that you find most useful and beneficial, in Dharma? And finally, if there was a complete newcomer to Dharma, what would you say to them, in one sentence, to sum up what Dharma is all about; to sum up the most essential thing?'

These were the three questions I asked and, of course, there were many different answers from different students. But there was one person who gave me an answer that I still remember. First, he said that the most difficult thing he found about Dharma, the thing he disliked the most, was that he had to do everything himself.

'I have to do everything, I have to be responsible, nobody can do it for me, I have to do it all myself. That is the most difficult part for me, and I often don't like it at all.'

Then he said, 'What I like the most, and what benefits me the most, is actually the same thing. I need to really be responsible, myself, and that is the most important thing in the end. Essentially, that is what has benefitted me the most.' Then he answered the third question, how would you describe Dharma to someone who is totally new to it? And he said, 'I would say exactly the same thing! - You are responsible for yourself.'

I thought this was kind of funny, but there is also a lot of truth in it. This is a key thing about Dharma, it is up to me: if I need to transform myself, I need to do it myself, it is up to me. If I need to become better at something, I need to train myself, I need to work on that. Buddha said, again and again, 'I show you the way. Whether you become liberated or not is up to you.' Dharma is the journey to become liberated.

We talk about two types of Dharma: one is the experience of an enlightened being, somebody who has transformed him or herself, who has developed his or her qualities and potentials fully; their experience is one kind of Dharma – the Dharma of experience. And the other type of Dharma is the teaching and guidance coming from that experience. These two are both the Dharma. When we talk about taking refuge in the Dharma, we are talking about deciding that you want to learn that Dharma and then that you put that into practice, deciding that you would like to tread on that path. When you decide to do that, that is going for refuge to the Dharma. This is very important because it is myself, working and training on it, that makes the difference. Guidance is important but without myself putting it into practice, it will not transform me.

Then there is going for refuge to the Sangha. Here Sangha means the 'Arya Sangha.' The word in Indian means a group, which can refer to any kind of group, but that is not the sangha meant here. Here it means the person or people who have the experience and understanding of Dharma. I need Sangha in order to access the Dharma, I need people from whom I could receive this teaching and guidance, who I could follow. This teaching is not just an intellectual kind of teaching, it is a practical teaching. You need to know how to do it yourself; therefore, you need somebody who has some experience of it.

Everywhere in Buddhism, much is said about finding the right kind of teacher. If you have to follow a teacher, then you should follow somebody who is genuine and good. This means somebody who is living according to what they are teaching. You don't have to do whatever they say – never! Otherwise, you would be in trouble! It is very easy to become corrupted. I know this because I experience everybody being very nice and kind to me; they invite me all over the world and I can visit any part of the world and it feels like going home to me, because the people are so friendly and welcoming to me. Now, this is because I am teaching Dharma and people like Dharma, so they think they like me. If I misunderstood and thought it was because I was so great, I was so wonderful, everybody likes me, I could easily become corrupted. It is not because I am great, I should not have that misunderstanding; it is because of Dharma. People like what they hear, the teachings, which I have learned to repeat. If I thought it was because I am so great, I could become corrupted and end up doing all sorts of bad things. Going for refuge to the Sangha means I allow myself to be influenced in a positive way, not in a negative way.

Once you go for refuge to these three refuges, you are on the path of Dharma. You are receiving guidance and teachings, and you can receive these or learn from anybody. You can learn from a very great master, very good people, from their way of doing things and their experience. But sometimes you can also learn from very bad people, how you should not do things. And sometimes, even somebody who has a lot of bad qualities and negative qualities, they can still have many true and helpful things to say. And you can learn from these. It is not that I can only learn from perfect people. I can learn from everywhere, but I should not follow the footsteps of those who are not being good.

We need to use our own intellect and wisdom mind to guide us. The ultimate teacher is ourselves. Finally, it is us: our mind, our wisdom. If I say this is the right teacher or teachings to follow, the right practice to do, who says that? Who makes that decision? It is myself. Nobody can make that decision for us. We have the capacity to know what is right and what is not right. So, we have to use that capacity; we cannot rely on anybody else. People say many things, if they are happy they may say you are great. If they are not happy, they may say bad things instead.

Therefore, going for refuge is not something *out there*, it is something *in me*. We say this prayer over and over in many places in Buddhism, like before teachings and before practice, because we need to remind ourselves again and again - What is my purpose in life? We have a short life. You may think life is long, but when you are older you will find out, life goes very quickly. And within this life, we have to live in a good way, in a way that is useful, good for ourselves and good for others. If I can develop my own positive qualities, that will be very good for myself. If I can do something helpful for others, that will be very good also.

So, I should do something that is useful, beneficial and helpful. If I can do that, I will have lived a purposeful life. In order to do that, I need to have some direction, I need to receive some positive influence. I should not totally waste my life. And we need to remind ourselves of this again and again. There is nothing wrong with enjoying myself, but if I only do that, maybe at the end of my life I would wonder, 'What have I really done in my life?' If nothing else, just to make myself proud of myself and feel positive about myself, I should do something purposeful and beneficial. That actually leads to the next aspect: Bodhicitta.

Compassion for ourselves and for others

I usually see Refuge as compassion for ourselves, and Bodhicitta as compassion for everybody else. Buddha is the teacher, the greatest, unexcelled teacher, who can teach us how to find a way to free ourselves from all our sufferings and pain and problems. He is not just a teacher to show us a few techniques in one or two small things, he can show us the way to completely transform ourselves and find the highest, lasting peace and happiness and well-being. So, when we say we take refuge in Buddha, Dharma and Sangha, having this intention simply means that I must love myself. I want the best thing for myself. I want myself to be liberated. I want to find a way to do that, to really help myself in the best way possible.

Buddha is seen as a teacher, but he can also be seen as a doctor; the most wise and compassionate and skilful doctor, a doctor who knows how to treat all kinds of different diseases and who has the intention to help everybody to become cured from their diseases. What the Buddha gives us is the Dharma, so Dharma is like the medicine. There could be a very great doctor, but if he or she does not have the correct medicine that is suitable to cure the disease that the patient has, then the patient cannot be cured. The Dharma is like that, the right kind of cure for each and every person, and each and every circumstance. After taking refuge in the Buddha, I therefore take refuge in the Dharma. If I find the best doctor but I don't take the medicine he or she gives me, or if I don't take the medicine as the doctor advises me to, I would not be cured from the disease.

Then, if I am very sick, I need somebody to take me to the doctor. I need people, like a nurse or an ambulance person or my friends, to help me. Somebody needs to put me and my doctor together, and me and my medicine together. That is the Sangha. Unless I have those people, who could help me with meeting the doctor, getting my medicine and getting all the necessary things together, I would not be cured. I need all these three things and so, taking refuge in Buddha, Dharma and Sangha means I care for myself, I want to liberate myself, I want the best for myself, I love myself.

Therefore, taking refuge is 'loving yourself' practice, compassion for yourself. It is doing something for yourself, and not in a small or limited way, but in a complete and big way. And that is possible because I have that possibility, I am curable. I have that nature. I have all the positive qualities within me. So that is taking refuge.

Now, every being is like me. Nobody is totally different. Everybody wants good things for themselves, everybody wants to be free from suffering and pain and problems. Therefore, they are all equal to me and so I would like to help them. I would not only like to do this for myself, I would like to do this for all sentient beings. I would like to commit myself to bringing lasting peace and happiness, which is Buddhahood, to all beings. I commit myself to working for that and I will not rest unless this happens. And for this, I make a promise. When you make such a promise or commitment or intention, from the depth of your heart, that is called generating Bodhicitta.

So, this is compassion for everybody. Seeing everybody as equal, similar to myself. I can stand in the shoes of everybody, irrespective of who or what these people are. All the beings throughout space, all different kinds of beings, human beings, non-human beings, they all are the same in terms of wanting peace and happiness. So, I would like to try and bring that to everybody, whether they are in a very good situation, better than myself, or whether they are much worse off than myself; whether they are doing nice helpful things at this time or whether they are doing very bad, negative things. I would like to bring the best for them, also.

Bodhicitta

What is the best way of making myself feel really useful? I am not talking about it 'being your duty to help everybody, so you must help everybody.' I am talking about myself, as a selfish person; a selfish, samsaric, egoistic person. What makes me feel worthy or useful, as if I am somebody who is a little bit important? The more I do something that is helping other people, the more important I am. If I do nothing, and help nobody, if I don't do anything that affects anybody in any way; then, who am I? I am nobody. But if I do something helpful, that really benefits somebody even in a small way, then I can feel good about myself. The more I do, the more worthy I become; the more important I become, the more useful my life becomes.

Whether people appreciate me or not is another thing. Whether people appreciate me or not depends on other people. What is more important is how I feel about myself. If I genuinely try to do something really helpful and useful for the world, then I would feel, for myself, that I have not wasted my life. I would feel some sense of purpose and worthiness.

The text is saying, 'All the sentient beings throughout space, I want them to be enlightened; I aspire for that, and so I generate Bodhicitta.' We are saying here that we want to help everybody, and to help them the best we possibly could. So, I should use my life to at least do the first step towards that. Even if I couldn't do much, at least if I have that intention, and I manage to do something even just to help myself, that is a good step to take. And that would make myself feel I have at least not wasted my life.

To make that intention or aspiration, therefore, becomes important. This is something that we try to train our mind towards: 'I wish I could help everybody. I wish I could help to reduce the pain and suffering of everybody. I wish I could get rid of the pain and problems of everybody, of course including myself.' And there are lots of problems in the world; there is a lot of pain and many problems in the world. I know this, I understand this; and I also know that there is nobody in the world who wants to suffer and have lots of pain and problems. So, if I can help even a little bit in this direction, it will be good for me and good for everybody.

So, I say a small prayer to pray for that. I pray that I may eventually be able to get rid of all the sufferings and pain of everybody, without exception. I pray that I may be able to bring lasting peace and lasting happiness to everyone. If I make that prayer, my heart has turned into a compassionate one. My heart has turned into a very generous, warm, kind and positive one. Even if there are lots of negative things and pain and problems going on all over the world, if I have this heart, there is a little, small, glowing thing present. So, this becomes a very important thing, what we sometimes call generating Bodhicitta. It's good for myself, good for the person next to me, good for people around me, and good for everybody, because there is no bad or negative wish there.

> kha nyam sem chen tham che kün
> sang gyä thob chir sem kye do
>
> *And I generate bodhicitta so that all beings, as limitless as space,*
> *May attain perfect Buddhahood.*

Therefore, even if I can't feel the whole potential of it, I still need to exercise and train, at least to say it. Because sometimes it is necessary to train with very small steps. Training is step-by-step, and sometimes those steps need to be very small. If I am just able to say, 'May all beings be free from suffering,' that is a start.

There is a story of how Buddha taught a method of training our generosity. I think this is a very good example. Anathapindika was one of the great sponsors of Buddha, but at the beginning he was not generous. He liked Buddha, he used to listen to his teachings and then go away. But one time, Buddha was talking about generosity, and after the teaching Anathapindika went up to Buddha and said, 'Well, I like you and I like your teachings, but this generosity business is not for me.'

Buddha said, 'Yes, but you can train yourself on it.'

But he said, 'No, I can't train, I don't want to train. To give something away feels like cutting a piece of my flesh off. I don't want to do that.'

And Buddha said, 'But you can give yourself something?'

'Yes, no problem with that!'

'Then you can start there. You go home and take something in your right hand, and then give it to your left hand and say, 'Take it!' And then give it back to your right hand and say, 'Take it!' You just do that. Keep saying 'Take it!''

I don't know if it really happened like that, but this is the story.

So, Anathapindika went home and took a piece of gold – he had many – and took it in his left hand and then offered it to his right hand, saying, 'Take it!' He knew he was not really giving anything away – he was just passing it to his other hand – but to say, 'Take it!' was still a little bit difficult, a little bit uncomfortable. He found it not so funny. But it became a little bit of a challenge, so he kept doing it: 'Take it! Take it!'

He was doing this for a while, when it suddenly occurred to him, maybe it would be nice to invite Buddha for lunch. So, he invited Buddha for lunch, and he gave Buddha lunch and he also had lunch and it was very nice; everybody enjoyed it. Then next time he was at a teaching, he thought, maybe I should invite Buddha and his monks for lunch. So, he did that and everybody was very happy. And that is how he gradually became very generous. He started opening free kitchens to everybody, building hostels for travellers, hospitals for animals; he built all kinds of things.

That is how we should train in Bodhicitta. First, we may just recite the words and feel nothing more. Then, we may start to feel something when we recite the words. And gradually we familiarise ourselves with this feeling and we start to feel a little bit more kind generally. Because there is no use or reason to have negative wishes towards anybody. If I have negative wishes towards anybody, it doesn't help me in any way. It is not nice to have negative feelings. When I have anger or bad feelings, or want something bad to happen to somebody, that is not a happy feeling. It is not good for me. Once I understand this, I can slowly train to develop Bodhicitta, and that is the training.

This is actually the most important part of the practice. We always need to inspire ourselves, again and again, and this is a very important way of inspiring ourselves, with Refuge and Bodhicitta. The more we clearly see this and clearly understand the purpose of practice, and the need for it, then I think we become more inspired to practice. It is traditional to start any teaching with a reminder of Bodhicitta, and the great masters always used to spend a lot of time on that. Like when Dilgo Khyentse Rinpoche taught, he always used to spend a lot of time on Bodhicitta, every session.

So, Refuge and Bodhicitta are the foundation of all practices. If these two are not there, as the basis, then all other things become like a play, just a game; they don't make much sense. If these two things are very clear and strong, as the foundation, then any practice or anything we do, would become a great practice, a Bodhisattva's practice: a great positive accumulation. So, when we say these first four lines, it is very short, but it is very deep. And it is good if you can reflect on the meaning for a little while. Saying it three times gives a bit of time to reflect on it, to allow it to really sink in deeper. That is why we usually say this part three times.

Experiencing the pure being within us

Next comes the actual practice and, in this practice, we visualise ourselves as White Tara. This visualising is called the Generation Stage or Creation Stage. But in the end, if you look deeply, the way we are, the way our mind is, the way our consciousness is, and the way Tara is, or the enlightened being is, is not different. In essence, it is the same thing. That is the main understanding underpinning the practice. The difference comes in the way we perceive.

The way we perceive is clouded by a lot of negativity, lots of negative emotions, lots of negative habitual tendencies, and a lot of delusion and ignorance. As a result, we are a samsaric being. If we were to change that state of mind, if we could see ourselves as we actually are, and see everything around us as it actually is, if we could be like that now, then we would be enlightened; we would be Buddha.

Gampopa said, 'Samsara is just a misunderstanding.' And this misunderstanding is about the whole way we see things. It is not just an intellectual understanding we are talking about, but an experiential understanding. Our mind is clear light, is enlightened, is clarity. But that clarity, we take it as 'I.' Then, because I take the clarity as 'I,' whatever manifests I say is 'out there.' Within that clarity there is actually no separation, no duality, no 'I' and no 'out there.' But I have made it into a duality. On the basis of that, all my reactions arise: 'That is nice for me.' 'That is not nice for me.' 'I want this.' 'I don't want that.' We react with aversion and attachment, and that is what makes samsara.

If we understood the awareness we have, the mind or consciousness we have, as clear light, as enlightened experience, pervading throughout, that would be the difference: Empty in nature, but everything manifesting from there. Then, there is nothing called 'there, outside' and 'here, inside.' We would not react with aversion and attachment. But, since that is not the case, we need to change our perception, we need to transform it. How can we do that? Firstly, we need to study, we need to get instructions. But then we also need to exercise or practise our experience. That is what this practice is: an exercise, a training, on that. To feel the pure being that is within us; the compassion, the wisdom, the clarity, the purity, the perfect energy that we have. That is what we need to experience.

A reminder of the ultimate nature of things

In order to do this, we start by reciting the mantra:

OM SHUNYATA JNANA BENDZA SOBHAVA ETMAKO HAM

This is a mantra that is written in Sanskrit. *OM* is usually at the beginning of every mantra. Sometimes people meditate purely on *OM*; this is a tradition, both in Hinduism and Buddhism. *OM* is sometimes described as the origin of all sounds. I had my own idea about this, I didn't see it anywhere else so maybe it is totally wrong, but I thought maybe it is linked to how, whenever we start to say something, we often start by saying 'Mmmmm' at the beginning.

What is traditionally said, though, is that *OM* is actually made of three sounds: *A-U-M*. That is why they say it represents the three kayas. You can chant *OM*, lengthening out the syllable, which can be very nice. It is one of the sounds associated with deep healing, and in this context it is associated with the body, healing of the body. In this kind of a practice, you can visualise *OM* above the crown of your head or inside your head – white, the colour of the moon. And then you recite *OM* very melodiously and feel that lights come from the *OM,* healing your whole body. All the negative things are purified and so forth.

In fact, healing usually has three components. First, purification: all the bad things, obstacles, negative things, illnesses and things like that are cleared, that is the purification. Second, healing: what is broken is joined, what is blocked is made flowing again, what is cut is made whole again. Third, transformation: healing means what has gone wrong has been made right, but transformation goes further than that. At the moment, maybe we call ourselves healthy when we don't have any problems. But when you are transformed, it is not only that you don't have any problems but that you feel completely healthy and completely nice and completely wonderful. That is called 'transformed.' So, you feel your body is experiencing all these three aspects of healing as you recite, again and again, with light rays coming from the *OM*. Also, then, those light rays go and heal others.

Here we simply have *OM* at the beginning of the mantra. Then *SHUNYATA*. *Shunyata* is emptiness. His Holiness the Dalai Lama was recently saying that, in order to understand emptiness, one must study physics. Without studying quantum physics, he was saying, one cannot understand emptiness. So, I don't know if I am qualified to say anything about it here! But, essentially, emptiness does not mean there is nothing there; it is about *how* things exist, that is *shunyata*. That is why interdependence and emptiness are said to be one and the same. You can say everything is interdependent, or you can say everything is emptiness, or *shunyata,* they mean the same thing. It is not that everything disappears when you understand *shunyata.* That is why, in the Heart Sutra, it says:

'Form is emptiness.
Emptiness is form.
Form is no other than emptiness.
Emptiness is no other than form.'

It is not about: because it is emptiness, you cannot touch it, or you cannot see it; it is not like that. Because we can touch it, because we can see it, the whole colourful world is there, because it is interdependently-arising, because its nature is emptiness. That is why it is there, and how it is changing all the time and it is still there. That is why so many things are possible. It's possible to grow, possible to disappear, possible to create something else. There is the possibility of chemistry; you can put two and two together and it becomes five, becomes something new. Intellectually we can understand this a little bit, but it is not easy to understand this experientially. That is where the problem lies. We are so used to holding everything very solidly and in 'one way.' It is very difficult to change that, which is why our mind is so stuck.

I am told that people catch small elephants and then they tie them, with a jute rope, to a peg. Not very strongly, but enough that the little elephant cannot pull away. And then the little elephant tries to pull and break away, but it cannot. So, then it realises it is not possible. But when the elephant becomes very big, and it could snap the rope in two very easily, because it is so powerful, you can still tie the elephant down with the same small rope. And it doesn't pull away because it thinks it is not possible to. That is the kind of frame of mind we have too. That mentality binds us and so, therefore, we get stuck.

All the aversion and attachment and fear we experience, come from this way of seeing, of not understanding how things really are. So, therefore, a true understanding of *shunyata* is very important. The more you understand it, the more you don't have to get stuck in one way of seeing. Usually we think, 'This is like this. Good is good. Bad is bad. I am like this. Everything is like this.' And then we tell the story, 'It happened like this, I am the victim,' and so forth. Our mind is set in a certain way, and it is very difficult to free ourselves from there. But when we have, even a little bit, of an understanding of *shunyata*, then I understand there is nothing concrete called 'what I am.' At the moment, we have a very strong sense that this is me, they are not me, I am totally independent, everything there is totally independent, everything exists on its own. I am affected by everything; if it is good, in a good way, if it is bad, in a bad way. So, we have this very strong, independent, 'existing on its own,' way of seeing.

When I see things in this way, that is how we have this samsaric state of mind. I may see something, or I may experience something as nice and I think, 'Oh this is nice for me, I want it, I need it, I should have it.' I try to get it, and I run after it again and again and again, until I have it. I feel that, if I don't get it, I cannot be happy, I cannot be satisfied. But the process of getting it is always full of a lot of trouble. Maybe I will get it; maybe I won't get it, I have fear of not getting it, hope of getting it, I'm about to get it, I'm not getting it. Maybe someone will get it before I get it; she has taken it; he has taken it. Even if I get it, it is not always happy.

I got what I was trying to get for a long time, sometimes with lots of difficulties, but many times I am disappointed. I find that this, what I was trying so hard to get, is not really what I wanted.

That happens many times, because we have huge expectations. Things look quite 'shiny' but when I actually have it, it's not as I expected. So, I could be very disappointed. We experience so much disappointment, all the time, because of our expectations. This is true in many ways, in our personal experience, in relationships, even people coming to Dharma. They come to Buddhist centres and get very disappointed, because they read a little bit about Dharma teaching about all these nice things like loving-kindness and compassion. And they think a Dharma centre will be so nice, full of all these lovely qualities. But when they come, the first person they meet is grouchy and just offers them a vegetable to eat.

Everything is like that in life. Even if what you get is nice, that doesn't take the problem away. Now you have an even bigger problem: I might lose this. I will probably lose this. How might I not lose it? You start to worry. And that worry does not finish until either you lose it, or you don't want it anymore. So, it didn't make you completely happy even if you got it. And if you lose it, then you have another problem: how to get it back!

So, the whole system of our way of reacting creates problems. This is what they call suffering in Buddhism. Because there is always either dissatisfaction, or fear, or worry, or the pain of loss or the struggle to get something. We see everything in this way. If we see something as nice we have all these problems. If we see something as not nice, we have the problem of how to get rid of it. I should not have this, I should get rid of it, I try to run away from it. Even if I don't have it, I have a fear of getting it. And that fear is there even if there is no chance of getting it. If I get it, then I am very unhappy, I have the pain of getting what I don't want. And that does not stop until I actually get rid of it, or I don't fear it anymore. Even if I get rid of it, I still have the fear of getting it back. So, there is no end to suffering. It is not because of things but because of my way of reacting to things.

If we look a little bit more deeply, though, at what I am - who am I? It's very difficult to really see. I say, 'I am Ringu Tulku,' but what is Ringu Tulku? This body? A scientist recently corrected me; I used to say our body is made up of seven billion cells, but he told me it is more like a hundred trillion cells (a trillion is a thousand billion). He told me something even more interesting: that 90% of these are bacteria - other beings. So, is that me? Am I bacteria? I like to think I am not bacteria. But apparently 90% of my body is bacteria. So, it's difficult to say this body is me. This body is more like a cosmos, in a way. And it changes all the time. It changes so fast. If I brush my skin, millions of cells go. They say that every seven years, all the cells of my body are replaced. There is not one left. So, I have changed my body fully, completely, nine times, maybe more.

So, then, what am I? My mind? If there is something called mind, other than my body, then where is it? What does it look like? We know there is awareness, there is consciousness. That is what we call 'me,' that consciousness that says, 'I know, I want, I feel.' But this consciousness is also two things. There is an awareness that knows, but if you look for how and where it is, you will never find anything. You will never find a location where my consciousness is, whether inside my body or outside my body. You cannot find any specific identification, like size or colour or form, or any specific way in which it exists. That is the nature of the mind. You cannot say it does not exist, because there is awareness. But if you look, there is nothing there. That is why it is described as awareness and emptiness, inseparable. There is awareness, but emptiness also.

And everything we experience is experienced through that mind. If I say, 'I am,' it is that mind that is saying that. If I say, 'I am not,' again it is that mind saying that. If I say, 'other,' it is also mind saying that. If I say, 'nice,' mind is saying that. If I say, 'not nice,' it is also mind. 'I want,' 'I don't want,' also mind. 'I am desperate and unhappy,' that is the mind saying that. 'I am very happy,' also the mind. 'All these things are existing there,' that is mind saying that. 'All these things are not existing,' also mind. 'All these people are useless,' mind is saying that. 'All these people are Buddhas,' mind is saying it. If I say, 'I am the worst person in the world,' or if I say, 'I am Tara,' that is also my mind saying that.

Your mind can say anything, it can almost create anything. How you are and how you feel, more or less, depends on what your mind says. It might say, 'I am so happy, so fortunate, everything is so nice.' Or at the same time, it could say, 'I am so unhappy, so unfortunate.' It doesn't depend on how things are.

The example of Tenga Rinpoche is very clear. Even though he had lost his eyes and his fingers, and one leg, he reported he was so happy because he had had no obstacles in his whole life. And I think he really felt like that, he was so happy all the time. Recently I even found out that, when he had to have his second leg amputated, he had it done without anaesthesia. The doctors insisted he have anaesthesia because, even regardless of the pain, they said it would be very bloody and they had to use powerful machinery. But he said it was okay and asked them not to tell anybody, not even the monks attending him. After the procedure was completed, all the doctors and nurses returned and prostrated to him. It shows how it is all about how you look at things and how deep the understanding of *shunyata* can go.

When you deeply understand what it is that you are, and your relationship to everything, then you see everything as manifestations of interdependence; and you see how everything is changing. We say that 'I am this,' and I am separate from everything, but then I can't even identify what exactly is 'me.' Even my body is totally dependent on everything around me. If there is no air for me to breathe, how long would I last? Maybe five minutes, maybe not even that. And if there is no heat around me, if there is no water? My existence is dependent on everything around me, on all the elements. I don't exist without those things. Therefore, I am not totally separate from them.

Then we have all these things I feel I need, that I have to own. Actually, can we even own anything, practically? It is just a kind of concept. To understand this nature is important, therefore. The more clearly I understand this, the more I have less fear, the more I have less anxiety, the less I feel 'it should be like this, it must not be like this.' So, more and more, I can let things be; I can do without expectations. I can live more happily and experience more joy, because whatever happens it is kind of okay. It doesn't mean I cannot do anything to improve things, I should still do things. I should work, I should think; if something I want to happen goes well, I can be happy. But if it does not go well, I can still be happy, because I can let it be. Even a little bit of understanding this *shunyata*, therefore, can change my way of reacting to things.

Then *JNANA: Jnana* is wisdom. This is not just intellectual understanding but experiential understanding of how things are interdependent, what dependently-arising really means, the emptiness nature of everything.

Then *VAJRA,* which Tibetans pronounce *BENDZA,* is sometimes translated as 'diamond-like,' but what it really is, is a mythological implement which is supposed to be impregnable and indestructible. It was the weapon of Indra, the king of the gods, and could destroy anything, but nothing could destroy it. That is *vajra*. *Vajra* represents what you become if you have the understanding of *shunyata*. You become indestructible, because nothing can really harm you.

SOBHAVA means 'naturally,' not something we need to cultivate, it is already there. So, it means how things naturally are. *ETMAKO HAM* means 'this is the way it is,' 'this is how it should be,' 'this is the natural state of things.'

So, this mantra is saying how the nature of ourselves and everything is: wisdom and emptiness, and the unchanging nature of that; there is nothing other than that. It is a kind of reminder of the ultimate nature of everything. In a way, it is a quintessence of the whole wisdom part of the practice. You can call it Mahamudra. You can call it Madhyamika. You can call it the Ultimate View.

But understanding emptiness is not about saying, 'everything is emptiness,' because that is about imposing my idea of 'emptiness' on these things here. And that is not the way it is. If you really understand emptiness, you don't say, 'everything is emptiness,' because that is a concept. You would not say it. You understand that everything arises, everything is there, and everything happens and changes, but while everything is arising and changing there is no question of 'emptiness.' There is just manifesting. Any concept that I make, is my concept: It is not how things are. If I say, 'this is emptiness,' that is just an idea. If I say, 'this is not emptiness,' that is also an idea. So, how do I experience emptiness? The real experience of emptiness, as compared to talking about emptiness, could be as different as dark and light, totally opposite.

That is the problem here. Because we function conceptually. We are intellectual beings. We always talk and think and make concepts, but those concepts are not how things are. They are a little bit of explanation of how things are, but it is almost impossible to explain how things are using concepts. For example, if somebody had never tasted honey, and you wanted to explain how honey tasted, how could you do that? It is impossible.

This is illustrated well by the story of six blind men when they were asked to explain the elephant: Six blind men were taken to an elephant and were asked to explain what an elephant is like. So, they all touched the elephant and the one who touched the trunk said, 'Oh, an elephant is like a big snake.' The one who was touching the belly said, 'An elephant is like a wall.' The one who was touching the tail said, 'An elephant is like a rope.' This is how it happens; you cannot explain how things actually are in concepts. So, maybe it is useless for me to try here, also - it will be like a blind man trying to describe an elephant!

So, if you have some understanding or a little experience of what we are trying to describe here, you see things from that point of view. If you have nothing to go on, if you have never even heard of all these things, then you just dwell on space; let your mind rest in empty space.

The visualisation

tong pä ngang lä hung drä sung khor kar
Out of emptiness, by the power of the sound of HUNG,
Appears a white protection circle, like a huge tent.

We always use sounds in this way. Mantras are sounds. Even in the Bible, it says, 'In the beginning was the Word,' and 'Word' is sound. In all these visualisations, the sound comes first, the syllables. Sound and light are the basis of all genesis, the origin of how all things arise. So, here, we say *HUNG* and then feel this protection tent arise, made of white light. Most of these healing practices always have a protection tent. And it is often said that, if you are engaged in any kind of healing practice with others, it is important to feel this protection tent. It is all interdependent, as you know. So, therefore, if you can give something good, you can also give something bad; and you could also receive something bad. There is always this interaction. It is impossible that you would be able to not receive something, good things and bad things.

So, therefore, there is this protection tent. It is huge and spacious, made of white light and vajras; a vajra net behind the white light. Usually, for Tara, also made of flowers. Sometimes it can be made of fire as well, but not usually for Tara. Although it is made of light, it is impregnable. Nothing negative can come in. Only positive things can come in.

Sometimes we need to practise these things. We can practise *OM* healing, just meditating on *OM*, or reciting *OM*. It is a very good practice, and is supposed to be very good for your heart, for your throat and for all sorts of things. For people who are not so visually-orientated, but are more auditory, the sound is a very good meditation. And, in the same way, we can practise visualising the protection tent on its own, also. You feel there is nothing negative inside the protection tent. If you are working with other people, you can visualise them inside the tent also, but if you are doing a lot of this work, you can focus more on yourself. The main thing is to feel the presence of this protection.

Next, a very beautiful palace arises:

de ü dhrum lä chu shel shäl yä khang

In its centre, from the syllable DHRUM, appears a palace of white crystal.

All these things we visualise here are to create certain conditions. We always have a lot of attachments, to our body, to our home, and so on. So that our mind is habitually looking for something that is like a home or a house. We need to transform this attachment; our attachment for security, for a home, for a house, for a body. So, we exercise this ability to create whatever we want, wherever we are, instantaneously.

Just by saying *DHRUM,* we create this wonderful, spacious, luxurious and lovely palace. And in another moment, whoosh, it is gone; we dissolve it. We create it; we dissolve it; we create it; we dissolve it. And, through that, we reduce our attachment. It is the same with our body. We arise as Tara, or anybody, as a Buddha, as a great being, anything. Sometimes very nice and wonderful but not always so;

sometimes ferocious and ugly. There are wrathful deities, like Vajrakilaya, which are very scary looking.

Here we visualise a very beautiful palace, made of crystal, with many lakes and ponds and beautiful natural areas, full of flowers and birds. There is a beautiful fragrance to the place. As soon as you are there, you feel peaceful, joyful and uplifted. There is an aura of peace and harmony, completely healing, with everything transformed into wellness.

The palace is not the important thing; how we feel is the important thing, because all these things are to train our mind. If our mind is focused on something ugly, unpleasant, dark and claustrophobic, something very disturbing, then we are feeling that. If we focus our mind on something very wonderful and nice and beautiful, with very nice kind of energy, then we are feeling that. If we keep on feeling that positive aspect more and more, then that is what our habitual tendency to feel gradually becomes. So that we create a karmic condition to have that kind of experience more and more. That is the main idea.

> ü su pam lä pema a lä da
> *In the centre of the palace, appears a PAM,*
> *Which becomes a thousand-petalled lotus flower, with an A upon it.*
> *The A transforms into a moon disc,*

Then you say *PAM* and from that arises a very big, beautiful, special lotus flower, with a thousand petals. It is very fresh and immaculate, without any dust or dirt on it, completely unstained and unstainable. The lotus flower always symbolises something pure in India, something pure and immaculate and unstainable. They say there is some kind of chemical on the petals or the leaves of lotus flowers so that, even if they are growing in the dirtiest areas, they always look pure and undefiled. So the lotus flower has always been a symbol of complete purity, completely unstained.

You feel that flower and sometimes you can spend some time on these things. When you do the whole sadhana in a group, you might go through it kind of quickly. But that is not how we should always practise. When you are practising on your own, it is good to sometimes spend time over different parts. We talked already about spending time on *OM* or the protection circle. You can also spend time on the palace or the lotus flower. We spend time to see or feel – or even smell – a very nice, beautiful lotus flower. That can also be a practice.

Smell is supposed to be important. Sometimes people report having visions, of Buddhas or Bodhisattvas or Deities, but sometimes these visions are not true visions, they are obstacles instead. And sometimes they are just our own hallucinations. So, how can you tell whether something is a genuine vision, or a hallucination, or a negative force or obstacle? They say one of the easiest ways of distinguishing these three, is by the smell. If it is accompanied by a bad smell, like when somebody has eaten garlic, then you can tell there is negative energy. If there is no smell, then it is your own hallucination. And if there is an especially nice smell, then it is a real vision.

Then, from the sound *A,* arises a moon disc on top of that lotus. It is kind of a seat, a round disc, which has the colour of the moon. And then on top of that, you feel that your consciousness arises there, in the form of a white syllable *TAM.*

This is the moment when you arrive in the visualisation. If you find it difficult to visualise a *TAM*, you can visualise white light or something like that. The reason *TAM* is here is because *TAM* is the seed syllable of Tara and here it is a White Tara visualisation, so the *TAM* is white, the colour of the moon.

The *TAM* is transparent. It is your consciousness, your awareness, yourself. Although our mind does not have a form – we can never find a specific form for our mind – we always feel we have a form. Now we have this body. In dreams, we have a dream body. We always feel that there is a body. It is said that when you are dead and you are in the Bardo, still you feel that you have a body; this is called the Bardo body. All the time, wherever we are and in whatever situation we are in, we feel that we have some kind of a form. And what kind of a form we associate ourselves with, makes a big difference to how we are. So, therefore, whatever form we assume, we also assume that kind of a mental state. Many times, we are very stuck with the form we assume. For example, 'I am like this. I am the fat guy.' We completely identify with that form. When I am a little bit fat, I don't say, 'My body is fat.' I say, 'I am fat.' Although, fat is very good, from my point of view. We Tibetans like a little bit fat.

Two radiances

Next comes an important part, which we call the two radiances, or two radiations. There is your consciousness as *TAM*, with light radiating from it. Then you feel that lots of lights radiate from there, like the sun's rays, in all ten directions. These include the four directions, the four sub-directions and up and down and basically means everywhere. So, lights radiate everywhere, and you feel that they not only go through the whole world, but through limitless worlds, throughout space. And these touch all the enlightened and great beings. When we talk about enlightened beings, we are not talking about 'Buddhist' enlightened beings, because at the level of enlightened beings there is no 'Buddhist' or 'non-Buddhist.'

The light touches every enlightened being and is like a request or invocation of their blessing. They are pleased, if you want to call it that, and send their blessings. You can call it blessings, or grace or positive energy. All this positive energy and these blessings and their power of healing are collected, and they come back in the form of light and enter into the *TAM*. You feel that now you have received the blessings and energy and wisdom and compassion and positive healing power of all enlightened and great beings. You feel that you have now become very pure and powerful and wise and compassionate. You feel that energy. That is the first radiance.

Then lights radiate a second time, and they touch all the beings - all the people throughout the world and then not only human beings but animals and all kinds of beings as well, including hell beings and hungry ghost beings; all beings. And when the light touches these beings, you feel that they are all purified, transformed and healed. So, you have sent this healing to everybody. This is important from the Buddhist point of view: you don't just send healing to one person; you send healing to everybody and everything. So, you feel that everything is healed, and everybody feels completely great, kind, compassionate, wise and joyful.

Then the light returns, and zooms into the syllable *TAM*. Now the *TAM* (your consciousness or yourself) is even more energised, because it has accomplished the two purposes. It has accomplished bringing the blessing or energy of all enlightened beings. And it has accomplished the transformation and healing of all sentient beings. This is also an important aspect. When I feel that everybody around me has become healed and well and enlightened, I cannot feel anything but healed myself.

One way of making myself feel healed is not to make myself healed but everybody healed. If I feel that everybody is kind and compassionate, then there is no way I can feel unkind. There is need to think, 'I have to feel compassionate; I have to feel compassionate.' And keep checking if I am feeling compassionate enough. If I feel that everybody is compassionate, then naturally I feel compassionate. And I don't have to worry or say whether I am feeling compassionate or not. That is the skilful means here.

The two radiances are important because they are about purifying yourself; receiving the blessings and so on is very healing. This is another place where you can spend time during your practice - on the two radiances. Take time to do one thing at a time. You don't have to finish the whole sadhana every time.

rang sem tam kar yong gyur utpala
tam gyi tsen lä ö thrö dön nyi jä
yong gyur rang nyi yi shin khor lo ni

And on this moon disc, my own mind appears as a white TAM,
Which then transforms into an utpala flower, with my mind as TAM in its centre.
The TAM radiates light, bringing in the blessings of Tara and all the Enlightened Beings.
The light radiates a second time, transforming, healing and purifying all the

beings of the Six Realms.
In this way, the two purposes are accomplished.
The light dissolves back into the TAM, instantly transforming me into White Tara, the Wish-Fulfilling Wheel.

White Tara

So now, because of the two radiances and the accomplishment of the two purposes - receiving all the blessings and then benefitting and healing all the beings - the *TAM* is very energised and transforms to become White Tara. Now you see yourself as White Tara; you arise as White Tara. She is the colour of the moon, white.

chu shel tar kar shäl chig chag nyi pa
yä pä chog jin yön pä utpal dzin
shap nyi kyil trung rin chen gyen gyi trä
dar gyi sham thab da war gyab ten pä

White, like crystal, with one face and two hands,
Adorned with precious jewels and a lower garment of silk,
Her right hand is in the mudra of supreme giving, the left holds an utpala flower.
Her legs are in vajra posture; her back is supported by a moon disc.

The mudra of the left hand is called the mudra of the Three Jewels. And this hand is holding the stem of a white utpala flower, the bloom of which is at the level of the ear. In fact, there are usually three blooms. One is open, in full bloom; one is over, already going to seed; and one is in bud, about to bloom. These represent the Buddhas of all the past, present and future.

It is up to you how many of these details you want to include. But the important thing is the image is made of light, transparent, yet alive with wisdom and compassion. The face is smiling; the eyes are compassion and kind, beaming with wisdom and compassion and healing power. There is a back rest like a moon, and she is sitting crossed-legged, in vajra posture, or it is also called lotus posture. And she is very beautiful and youthful. She is attired like a princess. Buddha is portrayed in monk's robes, like an ascetic, which is about trying to purify oneself. But here, we don't need to do that because Tara is already transformed. You don't have to purify or get rid of anything. That is already accomplished. So, she is ornamented like a princess. There are thirteen kinds of ornaments, and she is wearing silk clothing. This is all in the Indian style. They usually wear three necklaces of different lengths and then they have bracelets, armlets, anklets, earrings and so forth. The details do not matter too much.

Then she has seven eyes, these are important. Three in the face, the two usual eyes and then the third eye, or wisdom eye. It is usually said that everybody has the capacity to have the third eye. People also talk about 'five eyes.' The idea with all of these is that our mind is naturally very clear, meaning that it has the capacity to see, or to know, beyond the time and distance you are in. At the moment, maybe we don't have that capacity, because our mind is too polluted and unclear. If it becomes unpolluted, and clear, then we can have the capacity to know through time and space: you can know what happened to the limitless past and what might happen to the limitless future, and also what is happening across distance, to a long distance. That is the natural capacity of the mind. So, when you are enlightened, then that capacity is realised or awakened. The third eye represents that.

That is what our meditation is also for, because our mind is too busy and too distracted and too unstable, so it is polluted by all of this and has lost that capacity. It is like when water is polluted and very much mixed with mud and sand and all kinds of things, then it looks very murky, you cannot see through it, and it is not good to drink. But the real, true nature of the water is not that. So, if you allow this same water to calm down and become undisturbed, the true nature of the water comes out, as all the pollutants naturally settle out of the water. This is what we do when we meditate, we allow our mind to relax, to calm down and settle and be undisturbed; so that, slowly, slowly, the natural quality of our mind comes out.

From the Buddhist point of view, some people have more of this 'intuitive' power, and some people have less. Some people can see the future and some people can see what is going on in other places. That is said to be a natural quality of our mind, which is sometimes stronger and sometimes less strong. So, it is said that when you meditate in a better way, then you can see everything, maybe you can see what everybody is thinking – it's not very pleasant if you are in front of those kinds of people! Some of my own teachers were like that. You have to be very careful all the time. Of course, they wouldn't say anything, but you still notice that they see. And usually it is said that, if you really want to teach and guide people, you have to attain that quality. Only then, can you truly guide people.

So, Tara has seven eyes. As well as the three in the face, there are two eyes on the palms of the hands and two eyes on the soles of the feet. And these symbolise that she can see everywhere, all her eyes are open. Like we already said, though, you don't have to visualise her in a Tibetan style. You can see her in a Western way, or as a mixture, whatever way you like.

In the three cakras, at the forehead, in the throat and in the heart centre, there are the three syllables, all very small: a white *OM* in the head, a red *AH* in the throat, and a blue *HUNG* in the heart. Sometimes we talk about seven cakras, or five cakras, but usually we concentrate on these three cakras. When you concentrate your mind on these cakras, they are activated, and it is helpful to open or activate these cakras. That is why there is a practice to concentrate or focus the mind on these three cakras. So, you feel these letters or syllables in the centre of each of the cakras. These three represent body, speech and mind, and actually you *are* body, speech and mind. So, if we can purify body, speech and mind, then you are purified. Therefore, sometimes, to make it very concise, these three cakras are sufficient. It is also possible to focus on more cakras.

Now, here is the meditation. This is all meditation but just to mention some aspects of it. If your mind is in a normal kind of state, then you can see the whole of Tara in your mind. But if your mind feels not very concentrated, then you can focus on one specific area of Tara, like her face or her eyes or the three syllables *OM AH HUNG*. If your mind becomes a little bit dull, then go to the very tiny letters and focus more finely. If your mind is okay, then you can focus more broadly and relax more. We need our mind to change a little bit. Sometimes, it needs to become more relaxed, sometimes more focused. So, you can change what you focus on, to make it interesting, also. Sometimes, feel the energy of positiveness. Sometimes, just focus on one thing, like a flower or something like that. Sometimes, something moving, like the mantra turning, can be helpful, or radiating lights.

We sometimes feel that, when we meditate, then there should be no thoughts, a total silent blank. That doesn't happen usually. Because the nature of your mind is clear. It doesn't go blank very often - unless somebody hits you on the head! - but it is not necessary to go blank. That is not what we are trying to do. What we are trying to do, what we are allowing to happen, is to allow our mind to be in the natural state. Really relaxed, and a little bit aware. Because that is what our mind is, awareness. Our mind is nothing but an awareness, a knowing. And, in that awareness, you can have seeing awareness when you see something. You can have hearing awareness when a sound comes. You can smell something; you can feel something; a thought arises; an emotion arises; that's natural, there is no problem. That is how we are usually; we chat with someone, and then we hear something, or feel something, or see something.

We just need to be like that, nothing special. The only thing is that we are a little bit aware, aware of what is happening. Not trying to control anything. Just being aware... and aware... and relaxed. Letting our mind be in a natural state. Not too much 'meditating.' Sometimes, meditating is a problem because I say, 'I am *meditating*.' I am trying to do something that is not natural, or trying to be something I am not. That pretention of meditation is sometimes less meditation even than usual.

So, there are instructions like: 'no meditation.' Then they say, 'no distraction.' Usually when we are meditating we are trying not to get distracted but we can't get rid of distraction because we are making so much effort to get rid of it; we are trying to change how things are, manipulating things. But when you are just sitting there and are not manipulating things, you are just a little bit aware of what is going on, and then you are not distracted. So, then that is what you do.

You relax. If you see, no problem. If you hear, no problem. If a thought arises, no problem. If an emotion arises, no problem. Whatever happens, no problem. Just a little bit aware, and aware of that awareness. Relax. You are not doing anything special. You are just being yourself. You are not pretending something. You are not trying to change something. You are not trying to do something. You are not trying to get rid of something. You are not trying to achieve something. You are just learning to be, actually. When you can do that, then you can really rest. You are truly resting, truly being.

We are not trying to change things or disturb things. We are just being; being clear, being aware, actually being 'undisturbable.' What makes us disturbed? Because we think we will be disturbed. If there is a sound and you just let the sound be, it doesn't disturb you. Making a fuss about the sound is the 'being disturbed.' Sometimes we seek solitude in nature, but if you expect it to be quiet, you will be disappointed; it is so noisy in nature! Having nothing and nobody to disturb us, is not the point. Making everything silent so we are not disturbed, is not the point. The point is that we make ourselves undisturbable. Then, only, our mind is stable. If I can make my mind undisturbable, then my mind is stable.

To that end, I should not mind whatever thoughts or emotions or sensations come. And to do that, I need to learn that, if there is sound, it is okay. Let it come; let it go. If there is a thought, if I don't follow it, or build on it, but just allow it in a natural way, then I am not disturbed by it. Because our mind has the natural capacity for anything to arise. A thought comes up. An emotion arises. A concept forms. And so on. And they come; they go; they come; they go. That is why it is so beautiful. Whatever is happening, you just allow it to happen. It is not that we are trying not to see, or hear, or feel. No, we see or hear or feel whatever happens. But, at the same time, we are not grasping onto it, we are not building it up into something, we are not reacting. This is the important part of the meditation.

We are going through the visualisation here with a lot of details. In the beginning, it is not necessary to worry about the details. The feeling is the most important thing. Then, you can gradually bring in seeing the details and practise each part slowly to learn them. Once you know them, though, the practice does not take as long as it takes to talk about them and learn them. The details are also an exercise, though, a training to make our mind clear. The more we train our mind to be clear, the more we see the details, more vividly and more clearly. So, therefore, the details are included. And when we see and feel the details, it is more likely that our mind will not wander off and lose focus.

Empowering the visualisation

Then we have what we call bringing the *Jnanasattva*.

> nä sum dru sum thug ü pe da tam
> de lä o thrö ye she chen drang tim
>
> *In the three places, are the three syllables OM AH HUNG.*
> *In the heart centre, on a lotus and a moon disc, is the white TAM.*
> *Light radiates and invites the Jnanasattva, which dissolves into myself.*

So, there are lights radiating, mainly from the *TAM* in the heart centre, and they bring the real Taras, lots of Taras. Enlightened Beings are not like 'I am only Buddha Shakyamuni,' or 'I am only Tara.' It is not like that. The energy is the same. So, with that light we feel the actual Tara, the true wisdom and energy of Tara, is brought and enters into our visualisation. It is receiving another blessing, another purification, another entering into us of the energies to awaken our own Tara. So, it is bringing the *Jnanasattva*; *jnana* means wisdom here, and *sattva* is being. In Buddhist terminology, which is not that necessary actually, when you visualise yourself as Tara, that is called the *Samayasattva*. And then bringing the blessings in the form of Tara, which enter into you, and become inseparable from you; that is called bringing the *Jnanasattva*. So, you feel more enlightened.

In Tibetan we have the words *yeshe* and *sherab*. The Sanskrit word for *yeshe* is sometimes given as *jnana*, and *jnana* can mean many things. It can mean knowledge; it can mean wisdom. *She* means knowledge or awareness. And here that awareness is *yeshe*, not just *she*. *Ye* is a syllable which means primordial, from the beginning, pristine. So sometimes *yeshe* is translated as pristine awareness or primordial awareness; knowledge or wisdom that is naturally there right from the beginning. So *yeshe* means that. So, here, when we say lights radiate, they bring that kind of experience which is free from ignorance - that kind of wisdom.

The word wisdom may also not be a one hundred percent correct translation. But what we mean is what wise people have, which is not just knowledge, not just scholarship, not just information; but a deep understanding of how to solve problems. A person who is wise is someone who we would ask for advice and instructions because they know how to solve problems. Wisdom is that, not just knowledge or information, but an ability to see through problems and see how it is. *Yeshe* is about that.

Then, also, there is empowerment. Empowerment is none other than that: empowering you; giving you the authority, giving you the strength, the permission, the experience. You can choose how much you want to focus on these things, in how much detail.

lar yang ö thrö wang lha chen drang te
wang kur ku gang rig dag nang tha säl

Again, light radiates, inviting all the Empowerment Deities.
They grant empowerment and amrita fills my body.
The overflow at the crown of my head appears as Amitabha, Buddha of Boundless Light.

So, the lights now bring all the Enlightened Beings; peaceful, wrathful, male Buddhas, female Buddhas, Bodhisattvas, all. It's possible to make this very elaborate and detailed, but the essential aspect is that you feel that you receive nectar flowing, like you are given a bath. And you are kind of enthroned or empowered by it. It is about convincing yourself, again and again, 'I could be okay.' It is like when someone is enthroned as a King or Queen: before they are enthroned they are just another person. Maybe a prince or a princess, but not the king or queen. Then somebody brings that person and puts them on the throne, puts the crown on their head and somebody says something and gives them a sceptre and whatever else they do. And then everybody says, 'Now you are the King!' or 'Now you are the Queen!' And they feel, 'Yes, now I am the King,' 'Yes, now I am the Queen.' The process is empowering. So, this is a little bit like that. I feel myself to be empowered, so that now I can really act like Tara.

As the sign of your empowerment, then, you feel the Buddha Amitabha on top of your head. Buddha Amitabha is a red Buddha, sitting in meditation posture. Now we have the full visualisation of Tara, we try to feel a little bit like Tara, and feel pure, and feel free from all our negative emotions. We feel fully compassionate and whatever we imagine Enlightened Beings feel like. Mainly, we relax our mind and feel pure and kind. And we feel everybody else is also like this, the same way as ourselves. We feel that we are not affected by negative things.

We need to have some idea what we mean when we talk about Enlightened Beings or Bodhisattvas, like Tara. A Bodhisattva is like an unacquainted friend to everybody: even if you don't know him or her, they have the same feeling for you as if they were your best friend. There is no concept of a stranger with them. That is the Bodhisattva's way of seeing things. A Bodhisattva or Buddha may hate negative emotions and negative deeds, but they love those that experience negative emotions and do negative deeds, which means they love even the worst kinds of people. There is no question of Buddha being upset with you, that concept is not there in Buddhism. Buddhas and Bodhisattvas cannot punish anybody, there is no question of it, it is impossible. Who punishes? Nobody punishes, it is only yourself. This is the concept of karma. If you do something negative, it might have a negative effect, and that negative effect could come down on yourself. It could also cause problems for others, and that could come back to yourself worse, too. But Buddhas and Bodhisattvas have nothing to do with that.

It is not that you are less loved, or less cared for, by Buddhas and Bodhisattvas because you have done something wrong. A Bodhisattva is somebody who has unbiased, and unlimited, care and love towards everybody. This is how Tara would be. If you do something wrong or negative, it is not good and maybe you should stop, but it is not as if you would be less loved or cared for. That is why it is usually said that to have connections with Buddhas and Bodhisattvas is a very positive thing. So, we try to make those connections. That is why we pray to Buddhas and Bodhisattvas, or visualise them or think about them. So, while we are thinking about Tara and trying to make a connection with her, it is making a connection with a Bodhisattva, and a good one. A positive connection is very good but even a negative connection is said to be better, in the end, than not making a connection at all.

When Buddha became enlightened, he gave his first teaching to five people, and one of these five became liberated. And people asked Buddha later, 'Of all the people in the world, why did you give your first teaching to these five? And out of these five, why did this particular person get the first benefit or fruition of your teachings? Why did it happen like that?'

Buddha said, 'It's a question of dedication and connection.' And he told a very famous story. He said that a long time before, he had been a hermit, and he was meditating on patience, in the forest in the foothills of the Himalayas. At that time, there was a king in that area, who liked to hunt animals. He used to come and camp with his whole court, and then go hunting with his men, while his womenfolk would walk in the forest. One time the women came across this hermit meditating in the forest, and he was very nice-looking, kind and compassionate, so they made offerings to him and spent time with him. But one day the king came back early and demanded to know where everybody was. When he found all his queens with the hermit, he grew very angry and demanded of the hermit to know what he was doing.

'I am just meditating here,' said the hermit, 'I am meditating on patience.'

The king cried, 'We will see how your patience is!' and he took out his sword and cut the hermit into many pieces. So, he killed him.

As he lay there, dying, the hermit said, 'You killed me for no good reason, but I am not angry with you. I will make this prayer that, when I become enlightened, you will be the first one to benefit from it. At that time, I will cut off all your negativities just as you have cut my body now.' And then he died.

Then, of course, because of this very negative action, this king had to suffer a lot. He was born into many different realms and so on until finally, when this hermit became Buddha, he was the first one to attain the full result of it. This story shows that even a bad relationship with a Bodhisattva becomes a good thing in the end. But the main point here is how to feel when you are visualising yourself as Tara, how to have some idea of what such a Bodhisattva is really like.

Mantra recitation

So now we have come to the mantra recitation of Tara. We visualise the mantras in the heart centre of Tara, above the blue *HUNG*, which we already talked about, in the heart centre. You can start simply with a white *TAM*, but then later can add a white wheel, which is hollow and has eight spokes. This wheel rests horizontally on a lotus and a moon disc. In the centre of the hollow wheel is the white *TAM;* above that is *OM,* and below it is *HA*. Then, the other syllables of the short Tara mantra are arranged on the eight spokes: *TA RE TU TTA RE TU RE SO.* Inside that, around the *TAM,* are the syllables of the long mantra. The long mantra is: *OM TARE TUTTARE TURE MAMA AYUH PUNYE JNANA PUKTIM KURU SOHA.* To see just the ten-syllable mantra is okay, but then of course you may not see that clearly either, so then just feel that it is there.

The syllables of the mantras are facing inside and placed anti-clockwise so that you could read them from the inside. If they were to turn, they would turn clockwise. The letters are very small, as if written with one hair. If you can't visualise them very clearly, it doesn't matter; you start by feeling the mantra in your heart centre.

thug ü pe dar khor lo tsib gye ter
teng og om ha ü su tam yig kar
mu khyü nang mar ngag kyi threng wa dang
tsib gye teng du yi ge gye chä säl

de lä ö thrö jung ngä dang ma dü
lar yang ö thrö lha dang drang song dang
rig dzin nam kyi tse yi ngö drub dü
lar thrö sang gyä jang sem jin lab dang
tse yi ngö drub dü nä tam la thim
chi me tse yi ngö drub thob par gyur

In the heart centre, on the lotus and moon disc,
Is a hollow white wheel with eight spokes.
In the centre of the wheel, is the seed syllable TAM, with OM above and HA below.
Around the inner circle of the wheel, stands the mantra garland, radiating light.

The light radiates through the vastness of space, gathering the pure essences of all the Five Elements, which dissolve into myself.
Again, light radiates, collecting the blessings and long-life siddhis of all the enlightened and worldly deities, gods, Vidyadharas and rishis who have accomplished long-life practice.
Light radiates a third time, inviting the completely enlightened blessings and siddhis of all the Buddhas and Bodhisattvas to dissolve into the TAM.
Thus, the siddhi of deathless life is accomplished.

OM TARE TUTTARE TURE SOHA

OM TARE TUTTARE TURE MAMA AYUH PUNYE JNANA PUKTIM KURU SOHA

This is the healing part. While you recite the mantra, lights radiate from it, and they bring the essence of the Five Elements. Everything that is in the world is made of five elements. These are usually said to be: Earth, Water, Fire, Wind and Space. But it is not only that, these are the gross five elements; there is also the essence of the five elements. For example, anything that makes things stable, is the Earth element. Anything that holds things together, is the Water element. Anything that ripens things, that brings the energy of ripening, is the Fire element. The Wind element is anything that makes things move, or grow. The Space element is anything that makes space. So, there is nothing that is living that is not made of five elements. Each of our cells has five elements. Any living being, or living thing, has to have five elements. And these elements have to be in harmony. When these five elements are not in harmony, things don't work, things get rotten, disintegrate, and die. They cannot live.

Therefore, for us, our life is dependent on the five elements; every cells needs five elements, our whole body needs five elements, every system needs five elements. So, you feel that this light that radiates out, brings back the pure essence of the five elements. It brings that back and it enters into us. This is the healing. Any illness that we have is because our elements are not in balance, so as soon as the five elements become balanced, that illness is healed. We feel we become healed and well; every cell of our body is energised and restored.

Sometimes people might wonder if it truly helps, just thinking about this or trying to feel it. But, actually, all healing in the world is nothing other than that: us feeling healed. The mind is very powerful. I even heard of an experiment some scientists did where they showed that just thinking about running has the same effect on your brain as actually running.

Lights then radiate again, and bring the blessing and positive influence of all the great beings who have accomplished long life; like devas, long-life gods, and great rishis and Vidyadharas, or anybody who has accomplished this. Blessing is a little bit like a cold, I sometimes say. If one person gets it and then they sneeze, they can give it to everybody! Similarly, if a person has very positive energies, it is said that you can get that blessing if you are in connection with it. This is the basis of pilgrimage and all these kinds of things. If a place was used by very highly realised people, it can hold that positive energy too. So, we try to receive these blessings and feel that these are received.

So, first there is the five elements; next there are the blessings of those who are not fully enlightened but who have very positive energies. Then, all the fully Enlightened Beings' blessings and energies come and dissolve into the *TAM*.

First you visualise this healing going to yourself and you feel yourself receiving it. Then you send it also to anyone you want to send healing to. We include our loved ones and our parents and so on, eventually all beings, and allow the healing to radiate to everyone. We also offer healing to our teachers and great and positive beings like His Holiness Dalai Lama and His Holiness Karmapa. Because, if we have very strong, positive beings amongst us on this Earth, that makes our world much better. So, for our own good, and for the good of the world, we do that. If we offer healing and longevity to great beings, it may help them, but it also helps us, because we are not receiving the healing only for ourselves, but also for others, including great, positive beings.

So, we feel that we have attained the accomplishment of wellness and longevity. And we feel that all those beings to whom we want to give health and well-being and longevity, they have also received that. And, within that visualisation, within that feeling, we say the mantra.

The meaning of the mantra is not so important, usually. But, to say a little: *TARE* is calling Tara. Tara is the name, but Sanskrit is a very complicated language – every word has at least 28 forms – and *Tare* is how to say it when you're calling. So, it is calling Tara and asking her to please liberate, or deliver, us from the negative things. *TUTTARE* is liberating us from all kinds of fears and problems and dangers. Tara is particularly said to liberate from the Eight Fears, or eight kinds of danger and problems. These are the fears, or dangers, of:

Lion	*representing*	arrogance or pride
Elephant		ignorance
Fire		hatred
Snake		jealousy
Thieves		false or wrong views
Ghosts		doubt
Ocean		attachment
Shackles		greed

Then *TURE* is also freeing from illnesses and all kinds of diseases. *OM* and *SOHA*, or *SWAHA*, are always at the beginning and end of mantras. There are different translations of *SOHA* but Tibetan translators usually describe the *SOHA* at the end of mantras like this as meaning: 'May it be in that way, stabilised, established like that. May it become true.'

When you are reciting mantras, you can do it in four different ways. You can sing it, especially if you have a good voice. (If you have a bad voice, then maybe sing it a little less loudly!) Another way is to say it out loud. Another way is to hum it, like a bee buzzing. And then, also, you can say it in your mind. As we said before, some people do say that, if you sing, not just mantras but anything, it can help your mind become more positive.

When you say the mantra, here, this is meditation. Sometimes you can focus on the *TAM* as you say the mantra, allowing your mind to relax on the *TAM*. Or you can see the whole mantra as you recite. Or you can concentrate more on the sound of the mantra, and let your mind relax in the sound. These are all meditation, just using different ways. Sometimes you can focus on the radiating lights, and feeling the receiving of the blessings and healing. Sometimes you can simply let your mind be totally natural, not doing any of these, and just say the mantra, or not say the mantra. These are the methods of meditation.

Sometimes you can feel you are Tara and all of this, and sometimes you can forget about it all and allow your mind to be in its natural state, not grasping on to anything, like the experience of Mahamudra. Aware, but with nothing to be aware of and no one to be aware. You can choose which method to use, according to your state of mind. If you are too inwardly focused, there can be a danger of your mind becoming dull, so if that is the case, you can let your mind concentrate more outwardly and become more spacious. When your mind is too much outwardly focused and scattered, then it can be good to centre the mind.

Sometimes you can feel your mind or awareness is like space or like the sky, and whatever thoughts or emotions arise, they are just like how clouds and sunshine and storms and rain arise in the sky. Whatever happens, none of these harm or disturb the sky, because the sky is limitless, and there is nothing there to be disturbed. That is how we have to understand our mind: it is just awareness and there are no limitations. So, therefore, there is nothing that can actually be disturbed. If we can look at our mind, or feel our mind, or awareness, to be like space; then anything that arises in it, cannot harm or disturb our mind. A thought or emotion or perception can arise; it comes up, arises within the mind, and dissolves within the mind. It doesn't come from anywhere; it arises in our mind. It doesn't go anywhere; it dissolves in our mind.

If we can allow that, we don't have to run away from anything and we don't have to run after anything, and if we can remain like that, then we can be undisturbed. We can let all these thoughts and emotions, and any kind of things, liberate by themselves. Sometimes we call it 'self-liberate,' because whatever arises, it's okay; it arises by itself and it dissolves by itself. We don't need to do anything. We don't need to work on it, or try to do anything. It dissolves by itself, so it is called self-liberating.

If we have the wisdom to know how to let things be, then everything is self-liberated. That is how the more highly-realised people deal with things. They know how to deal with things because they know the nature of their life. They don't have to fight with things. They don't have to struggle. They don't have to run away or run after things. So, if we can understand that, then we can also practise that way.

Then, you can also recite the long mantra. The special White Tara, long life, mantra is *OM TARE TUTTARE TURE MAMA AYUH PUNYE JNANA PUKTIM KURU SOHA*. We already said what the first part means. Then, *MAMA* means 'me' or 'mine.' *AYUH* means 'life.' *PUNYE* means 'positivity' or 'virtue.' *JNANA* means 'wisdom.' *PUKTIM KURU* means 'may it develop' or 'may it blossom.' So: 'May my life, virtue and wisdom blossom.'

Usually, the main focus is on the short Tara mantra and then, at the end, you recite the long mantra. The long mantra is especially for long life, development of your positive qualities, and also for healing - receiving the healing and sending the healing to others. You can do however much you want to do, but usually more recitations of the short mantra and a little fewer of the long mantra.

What I have described so far is the practice that is described in this text for this stage. But there are three visualisations we can do during mantra recitation. This described so far, is the first (with its three parts). Secondly, we can do the Six Protection Lights practice. And thirdly, we can include Amitabha visualisation. [See Appendix for these practices.] You can do these second and third practices if you want to, but they are also not necessary to do. At the beginning, it is better to concentrate on the first part, and bring in the second and third parts later.

Dissolution and Completion

There are two sides to our visualisation of Tara in this practice, in keeping with all Vajrayana practices of this type: generation and dissolution. Generation is when we are visualising and the visualisation is created. Dissolution is when it then dissolves. This is actually trying to work on our experience of birth and death. Generally speaking, it is understood that, in our life, there are two most traumatic things. One is birth and one is death. Sometimes it is said that birth can be more traumatic than death.

From the Buddhist point of view, most of our traumas come from our experience of birth and death, that is where they originate from. So, therefore, in order to solve this problem, we need to find a way of going through death and of being born, without this kind of traumatic experience. The Vajrayana, we have already said, is about working on our habitual tendencies. So, we need a way to work on taking birth, arising, without trauma, and also dissolving, or dying, without trauma. That is what these two sides of the practice are.

At the beginning, when Tara arises, there is no problem. From the palace, with the lotus flower inside it and the seed syllable upon it; from the different activities of that *TAM,* then Tara arises. So, in the same way, when you dissolve at the end, everything dissolves. We try to exercise arising nicely, without any problem, with lots of blessings and benefit, and dissolving without any problem. Once His Holiness the Dalai Lama said he exercises dying and being born six times a day, and this is what he was talking about. So, how to do that?

nö chü ö shu sung khor shäl yä khang
rang la thim shing rang yang tam la thim
tam yang ö shu ma chö nyug mä ngang
rang bab so mä long du nyam par shag

The container and the contained, the whole universe and all beings, melt into light and dissolve into the protection circle.
The circle melts into the crystal palace and the crystal palace melts into myself as White Tara.
Tara dissolves into the seed syllable TAM and the TAM itself slowly dissolves, from the bottom of the lotus flower to the tip of the nadi, and melts into light.
I allow my mind to rest in its original purity,
And remain, freshly settled, in the uncontrived, natural space.

When we would like to end our session, we feel that the whole world, the whole universe, dissolves. From the outside, inwards, it disappears. All the beings also dissolve, into light. And all this dissolves into our Six Protection Lights, and the Six Lights into the protection tent [see Appendix]. The protection tent dissolves into the palace, the palace dissolves, and everything dissolves into Tara. Tara then also dissolves, from the outside, until only *TAM* remains. And *TAM* dissolves, from the base upwards, until it dissolves completely. Nothing remains.

When everything dissolves there is nothing to hold on to. And you allow your mind, your consciousness, to be in that natural freshness. Let it be, and remain in that state of pristine awareness or natural, unfabricated state as long as you can. That is the dissolution.

Then, when thoughts start to appear, you arise again as Tara.

lar yang je tsün phag mä ku ru dang

Once again, I arise in the form of Noble Tara.

You simply appear as Tara without going through all the process. And, after making your dedication, you go about your day in that way. This dissolution is done at the end of every session. It is important to have this understanding, and experience, that you can arise as the most wonderful thing, but it can also dissolve, and that is no problem. Whatever nice things, or not-nice things, arise, or whatever experiences happen, they arise and they dissolve. So, therefore, we don't need to get attached, and we don't need to have fear and aversion, to anything. Because everything arises and dissolves. It dissolves and then arises.

That is the understanding. And we practise to try and experience that understanding. All this visualisation or meditation is about that, because meditation is not about thinking, but about feeling. We allow our mind to actually go through that experience, and thereby train in that experience. And both dissolution and generation, or arising, is what we call the Creation or Generation Stage. And then the Completion Stage is not the dissolution, but is about the view behind all this.

Either when we are alive, when we have the experience of being or birth or whatever, and when we have the experience of death, the nature of both, and the nature of everything is – as we discussed at the beginning – awareness and emptiness. Our mind is awareness and emptiness. All form is appearance and emptiness. All sound is resounding in emptiness. So, therefore, anything can happen.

Anything can arise, whether it is a form, very colourful, very beautiful, or sometimes very fearsome; whatever forms arise, even when they are there, they are emptiness and appearance. The nature of everything is a little bit like a dream, like a miracle, like a rainbow. It can arise and dissolve at any time. It is momentary and impermanent. It appears as very real but there is nothing which cannot disappear when its causes are no longer there. Even something that appears as very solid is there due to many causes and conditions and many elements, and if even one of these changes, then the whole thing changes. That is the way that everything is.

Three Sacred Principles

After the dissolution, at the end of the session, at the end of any session, we always do the dedication. Any kind of Buddhist practice, especially Mahayana Buddhist practice, the Bodhisattva's practice, always has three aspects which we call the Three Sacred Principles. The first sacred principle is Bodhicitta, compassionate motivation, which we set with Refuge and Bodhicitta: I would like to do this practice in order to bring lasting peace and happiness to all beings, and also in order to help alleviate all their sufferings. For anything I do, that would be my ultimate goal. The stronger my motivation, the more people I do it for, the greater the result I wish for, the more limitless my compassion; all these make whatever practice I do stronger, and more powerful.

What I do, is only one element of how effective my practice is. I could do just a small thing, a simple meditation or a little bit of practice, but if I did that little thing with a very strong and very big aspiration or purpose, that would make that small action a big and powerful practice. Our motivation is, therefore, one element that decides how strong our practice is. So, it is a very important element and we should try to make it as big and as limitless and as compassionate, as possible.

Then, the second aspect of practice is what we call 'non-grasping;' we should do the actual practice without grasping. This is about our understanding of emptiness. The more we understand the nature of everything and the nature of ourselves, the more clearly we understand that, the stronger the practice is. Sometimes we can make a lot of effort, reciting many mantras, practising for many hours, concentrating hard, and maybe we think we have been doing lots of practice.

'I have been practising day and night…'. But that does not necessarily mean we have done a lot of practice. If I have some wisdom, even a little clarity about the nature of myself and the nature of things, that would make the practice one hundred thousand times stronger. Because the actual practice would be without grasping.

The third sacred principle, then, is dedication. After we have completed our practice, whether it is a little prayer or a little mantra recitation or some meditation, whether it is a big thing or a small thing, short or long; after we have done that practice, then it is important to dedicate it. Dedicating it is like investing it. Dedicating is like giving something. If you have some money, and you put it into the bank, then nobody can steal it from you, even if you go to the worst part of town. It is said that, if you do a positive thing and you dedicate it, that positive thing can never be undone, can never be wasted.

Otherwise, if you do a good thing and then do a bad thing, or if you do a good thing and then have a bad emotion, that can actually affect the good thing you did, and that good thing can be reduced or even destroyed. In the Bodhicharyavatara, it says that all the good things you may have done over a long, long time, can be destroyed by one instance of strong anger. For example, you may have a good friendship that has been cultivated over many years, but if you get very angry one time, it has the possibility of destroying that friendship.

So, therefore, the dedication at the end is important. And dedication is actually giving, sharing. Whatever result or effect might come from the little practice you have done, you give it, or dedicate it, for whatever. Once again, there is a skilful way of doing it. And this skilful way of doing it is to say: the little practice I have done now, together with all the positive things I have done in the past until now, and all the positive things I will do in the future, I take all of this together as one and I dedicate it for the best, most ultimate result. I dedicate it towards complete enlightenment, complete peace and happiness, for all the beings.

So, you dedicate it for the highest, biggest and longest-term project first. Sometimes this might seem like an impossible aspiration, but it is good to try and do impossible things. As Akong Rinpoche said, 'If it's not impossible, it's not worth doing!' Why not? Why not wish for the very best? Make the impossible, possible. At least there is nothing wrong in having the most impossible, best, wishes. So, dedicate for the most impossible, absolute best thing first. Then, you can work your way down from there if you want and wish: Until then, may there be peace in the world. May everybody be healthy, and happy, have no obstacles, and have long life. Whatever good things you want to wish, you can wish them. You can also dedicate for specific things and specific people, also.

The bigger, higher, more ultimate and limitless, the dedication - by that much, your practice becomes stronger and more powerful. Even if you do a little bit of practice, they say the benefit of it never gets exhausted, until all that you dedicated that practice for, becomes accomplished.

In this sadhana it is only one line:

ge wä sem chen sang gyä thob par shog

Through this merit, may all sentient beings attain Buddhahood.

You can also recite some long-life prayers at this point, like for His Holiness the Dalai Lama and His Holiness Karmapa. Then this is the end of this sadhana practice. This is a very concise sadhana of White Tara. There are other, longer ones, and much longer ones, but they are all, in essence, the same. It is just that some are more, or less, elaborate. If you have received the empowerment of White Tara, it covers all of these White Tara sadhanas.

Clarifying the Practice

The basis of all these Buddhist teachings, especially in the Vajrayana, is that essentially we are not something bad. We talk about *Buddhanature*, meaning that the way we actually are, the way our mind actually is, is not bad. The way we are is exactly the same as that of a fully enlightened Buddha. That is why we say we have Buddhanature. But don't mistake it as saying you are already Buddha – you are not Buddha *yet*! Or at least, we have not yet experienced the Buddhanature. Our Buddhanature is because how things are is how things are.

It is not that things are one way for us and a different way for Buddhas. How things are is how they are. They are interdependent, emptiness yet appearing. That is how things are. That is how our mind is also. But the difference is that Buddhas recognise and see how things are, *as they are*. They understand or see things as they really are. And we do not see things as they really are. We see things in a wrong way. The difference, therefore, is described in a simple word: a 'misunderstanding.'

The difference between a Buddha and us, is that Buddha has no misunderstanding or mis-concept, has no delusion. A Buddha sees things as they really are and sees themselves as they really are. And we do not see things as they really are and do not see ourselves as we really are. That is the only problem. So, the problem is very small. But to correct that problem, depends on us; how intelligent we are, how wise we are, how we see it. And it is not just about seeing it, because it is about how we feel, our experience. Because once we have a little bit of a wrong way of seeing things, then, on that assumption of how things are, we build up all our experiences and reactions and emotions. We create a world for ourselves; we create our own reality. And that reality is what we call Relative Truth. We have an experience and nobody can really show us it is not like that, because we really see it that way, we really feel like that and we really react that way.

We are completely used, and addicted in a way, to that way of seeing and feeling and reacting, and that is the problem. So, therefore, we have to learn experientially, and step by step, even very simple things. For example, the way we focus our mind. It is not very difficult to understand – it is actually very easy to understand – that, in our life, we have lots of positive, good, nice things and we have lots of not-so-nice, problematic, difficult things happening. We have all those things, good things and bad things. We also know that if our mind is more focussed on, and thinking about, those positive, nice things, we would be happier and much better off. And we know, if we concentrate on negative things and problems, it makes us unhappy, disturbed, afraid, upset and so on. But we do that all the time, we always focus on our problems and negative things in our life. And then we have lots of unhappy moments. And then we complain all the time. That is how we are. We can see these things very clearly and yet we remain like that. But it is possible to change.

There is no mystery, actually. It's very clear. The main thing is to see things as they really are. But to see things as they really are is not easy. For instance, we talked about emptiness, but emptiness is not about saying 'everything is emptiness.' It is more about learning how to be, without always running after and running away from things. Our samsaric way of reacting creates problems and suffering because of our very strong negative emotions, essentially of aversion and attachment. This does not mean we should not enjoy anything, or become completely jaded by life. Not at all. It is okay to be very clear about what is nice, beautiful, wonderful, and not-so-nice, not-so-great. The problem is we then make a next step. Rather than just enjoying something that is nice, and leave it at that, we start to want to get it or get more of it and so on.

I see a nice flower and then, instead of just enjoying this nice flower, I create lots of problems about it. I start to wonder, what about tomorrow? Or I say, 'This is a nice flower, but who owns it?' Does it really matter who owns it? Can I not just enjoy it? But we make things like that. 'It is *my* flower! Why don't you like my flower?' And so on. All this is a little bit not-so-intelligent. And that is what the problem is.

If we saw more clearly we would appreciate good things as they are, and not find it a problem when they are transient. Good things are transient. Bad things are also transient. None of this is a problem. If we really understood the nature of things, it is not so necessary that we have to be so strongly emotionally involved. This flower may come up and bloom and then pass, but then another one will come up. Same with me, same with today and tomorrow: today will go, but tomorrow will come.

Our real problem does not come from how things are, but from the strong negative emotions that come up when we get involved with things. I get upset, I get angry, I get unhappy and disturbed; I lose sleep and get high blood pressure; I get all kinds of problems in my body and mind; I get sick, and then I get more sick. Then I become so problematic, I make everybody around me sick too. Sometimes I make so much trouble that I make everybody around me fight each other, and that is how we bring all the suffering, pain and problems in the world. Sometimes, really for no reason. In the end, it is not how things are, but how we react, that is the problem.

Therefore, these negative emotions are what we need to change; whether they are anger and hatred and feeling hurt; or too much greed and clinging, dissatisfied and never content with anything, too attached and wanting things; or jealousy which is also a very difficult emotion; and our wrong ways of seeing things. These create our actions and activities and, in a way, our reality for ourselves. A wrong kind of reality, a deluded reality. And that is what we sometimes call *karma*. Karma is that: our actions because of these emotions. We are so much in it that it creates a reality for us. And we get stuck in that.

So, therefore, these practices are trying to change that. When you are feeling that you are Tara, you are not becoming somebody else. It is just that you are trying to experience the more pure aspect of yourself. You are just trying to experience your true, natural state; your true, natural way of being. Also, all the purifications that we visualise is to bring that feeling. In a way, there is nothing to purify; the only problem is a way of seeing. But we are so caught up in it all, we feel that there are lots of things to purify. So, therefore, we should feel that we are purified. Purification is also a kind of changing, freeing ourselves from these wrong and negative ways of seeing and thinking and feeling. Allowing those layers and layers of negative coverings to let go.

Further questions and answers

Posture

Student: How important is posture during meditation? I try and maintain a good sitting posture but sometimes, when I am tired, I do the practice lying down.

Rinpoche: Yes, they talk about posture and sometimes they say that posture is very important and sometimes they even say that, if you do the right posture, you don't need to do anything else. I think it is because the posture of the body also affects your mind, your channels and so on. Also, if you are sitting in that posture for a long time, and repeatedly, as people usually are for meditation, it is the same as if you do anything, whether sitting or walking or lying down, in the wrong posture for a long time; it is not healthy. That kind of thing can create lots of problems. So, therefore, good posture is recommended. But there are other postures, other than sitting, that are also recommended.

The main thing is that you can meditate in any posture which is okay for you. You can meditate while sitting. You can meditate while lying down. You can meditate while standing. You can meditate while walking. These are the four that are usually given and it means you can meditate in any way.

But this is a little bit like the story of the two Zen students. They were novice monks and one of them found the other smoking and cried out, 'Oh, you cannot smoke!'

'But I am meditating,' said the other.

'But you should not smoke while meditating. The teacher told me I should not smoke while meditating.'

'No, no, our teacher told me that I can meditate while smoking.'

'But I asked specifically. I said, can I smoke while meditating?' And he said no.'

'You didn't know how to ask him. I asked him and he said yes.'

'How did you ask him?'

'I said, can I meditate while smoking? And he said yes!'

So, maybe these things are a little bit to do with how you ask. You can use whatever posture is convenient. It is said that the future Buddha will be seated on a chair, and it is not made up by someone else, it was the Buddha himself who said that would be so. If we want to be in the sangha of the future Buddha, then, maybe we should learn how to sit on a chair. I sit on chairs often but I still have not learnt how to sit comfortably on a chair.

Visualising yourself as a woman if you are a man

Student: I find it hard to visualise myself as a woman, since I am male.

Rinpoche: We so much identify ourselves with gender. And, if I am a man, I am a man and nothing else. Or if I am a woman, I am a woman and nothing else. From the Buddhist point of view, this is nothing permanent, nothing exclusive. Every man has a feminine side. Every woman has a masculine side. And actually, you could be a man this time, but a woman next life. Or you could be a woman in this life and a man in the next life. There are instances of people remembering past lives that uphold this.

So, we should not be too fixed about gender. But maybe, also, this is a good opportunity to feel what it feels like to be a woman. Because actually men and women are so different.

Hand mudras

Student: When visualising ourselves as Tara, is it appropriate to take the posture her hands are depicted in? Because I noticed, if I change the angle or position of my hands, even slightly, it gives completely different information to my body. For example, the mudra of highest generosity gives my body certain information. So, is it appropriate to take these postures during the practice?

Rinpoche: There is nowhere that recommends you should do that, but I don't see anything wrong with it. These mudras are supposed to be a little bit significant. And mudras have a place in the practice. Some people say that different mudras are very healing. It is not a tradition that you would sit in that way while doing Tara, but there is no reason not to. When you teach, they do say you should assume the teaching mudra, which is another hand mudra.

Lights radiating

Student: When you are visualising the lights radiating, and the light is coming back to you, do you visualise that it is made of lots of small Taras; or is it just light that returns?

Rinpoche: In the beginning, when you do the two radiances, it's only light, no Taras. Then, when we bring in lots of Taras later, it is not only Taras that come, but all positive energies come. So, during the two radiances, you are just visualising light, not seeing any form within it. Then later, it is Taras made of light that come back to you, together with all positive energies, bringing the *Jnanasattva*.

Sounds

Student: When you visualise the protection circle arising from the sound of *HUNG,* and so on, where do these sounds come from, how do they sound?

Rinpoche: I think the sound is more like a natural sound. When there is wind blowing, there is sound. When there is a river flowing, there is sound. When the leaves are moving, there is sound. When there is fire, there is sound. When there is rain, there is sound. You can choose whatever kind of sound works for you. It is nowhere described exactly how the sound should be.

Purpose of visualisation

Student: Am I correct in thinking that one reason for elaborate visualisations is to occupy the ordinary, mundane mind so that the latent, wisdom mind can reveal itself?

Rinpoche: Basically, the visualisation is creating a focus or an object for your meditation. Almost nothing more than that. This focus is sometimes necessary because otherwise we don't know what is happening and our mind just goes all over the place and we don't even realise that is happening, until much later on, when we finally notice. So, the visualisation provides a reminder of something to come back to, like breathing also could. But, in the Vajrayana, we have an added aspect, like 'two for the price of one!' And that is that we are focussing on something pure. Which is what you were talking about.

Of course, you could say any meditation is a method to bring out our natural wisdom. So, in that way, all meditation is to do what you described. But here the extra aspect is to change our habit. It is more about habit than anything else, because our mind habitually goes to something negative. So, here, with the visualisation, maybe artificially or imaginatively, we are trying to engage our mind in a more positive way. Whether that is visually, or in our thoughts or feelings, or any other way, that is what is important.

Mantra turning

Student: Is the mantra turning in the visualisation or not?

Rinpoche: Not at the beginning. You can have the mantra turning later on, if you want, but I think it is important not to make things too complicated. Better to keep it simple. I am against all perfectionism, because that way things never get done.

Vipassana

Student: What is the Vipassana part in the sadhana practice?

Rinpoche: The Vipassana aspect of the practice is the view behind the practice. When we say the mantra OM SHUNYATA JNANA BENZA SOBHAVA ETMAKO HAM - that is the Vipassana part. And then it is the view behind the practice, the way you see things.

The protection tent

Student: I have a question about the protection tent – is it a protection for us, the one who is practising?

Rinpoche: Yes, but we are also instructed to make it very big and very spacious, not small, not claustrophobic. It is very spacious, and everybody is in it, all that needs to be protected is within.

Sending healing to others

Student: If I want to send healing to another person during the White Tara practice, how do I do that?

Rinpoche: There are two ways. One is every time you are sending healing in the practice, which is many times over, from the point of the two radiances onwards, through all these different levels of healing; you can think of that person and send healing to them, and think of that person as healed. The other way is holding that person's energy inside your heart cakra while you are doing the practice, so they are receiving the healing in that way. When you radiate the Six Lights, if you are doing that, they also receive each of these healings or protections.

Different people need different approaches

Student: Often in Buddhism, the advice seems to be around simplifying our lives. And yet here we have so many different practices: one Tara, then two Taras, then 21 Taras, 108 Taras, and for each of them we have a different practice. I want to ask if it is really beneficial to have so many different possibilities and different ways of visualising?

Rinpoche: I don't know, but I agree with you that there are so many it can get confusing. I studied, at one time, in the Namgyal Institute of Tibetology in Sikkim and I was studying, for three years, all the different thangkas and the meanings of all the iconography. But if you ask me if I know all the different kinds of Taras, I cannot say I do! It is that many, and so it can be a bit confusing.

The main thing is, from the Buddhist point of view, that different people have different needs. So, therefore, the Buddhas or Bodhisattvas or great masters teach slightly different things for different people. Essentially it is all the same, but certain aspects are brought out differently. And those different aspects are very beneficial for particular people. That goes for many different things. So, in Buddhism we have different yanas, so many different approaches and traditions and lineages and philosophies and practices. It is regarded as useful, not because everybody needs to practice them all, but because different people need different things. So, the way we have many different approaches is regarded as something good. It is for the same reason that we have many different religions in the world, and it is the basis of what we call the Rimé movement or Rimé way of thinking.

Different people need different things, different remedies, like you can't just have one type of food. A restaurant cannot offer just one food. In the same way, you can't have just one medicine for everybody. Different people have different diseases, different problems, and so need different medicines. Everybody has different tastes and likes different foods. I think it is supposed to be taken like that.

How much blessing you receive is up to you

Student: Are reading transmissions and pointing-out instructions given online as potent as if we receive them in person?

Rinpoche: I don't know, but the main thing in a teaching is that you understand, that you get the message. When a Lama is giving a teaching, sometimes to many different people, it is not the case that everybody is getting the same teaching. Somebody like me might be sleeping, for example! Or somebody who is sitting right at the back, or who has a problem with their hearing, they may not hear all the teaching.

Of course, it is always helpful to communicate one-to-one for a very special teaching like the introduction to your own mind, because then you can talk directly to the person and they directly can ask questions back. Communication is much easier and more intimate, that is why it is recommended. But, even without considering online possibilities, it is not so easy to get this opportunity. Most of the great masters are very busy and even to get an interview with them for ten minutes is not easy. So, the reality is you might never get a good-enough opportunity to receive most of the instructions. So, therefore, we usually get these instructions in a group. If it is given in a group, then I think whether you give it in a temple, or in a hall with lots of people, or whether you give it through the internet, I am not sure there is too much difference. Either way, the teacher is teaching what he or she wants to teach, and the students are listening to that teaching. It depends, no doubt, from person to person and situation to situation.

When we talk about reading transmissions or empowerments, these are kind of blessings, basically. Of course, the ritual objects are there, and there are lots of ritual objects. But to place those ritual objects on the top of your head is never considered the main thing. At a usual kind of empowerment, those in the front row might get it on top of their head from the main Lama, those further back from someone else. But this is never considered that important. The main thing is the trust and the faith and the devotion of the student. How much blessing I receive, whether I am in front of the Lama or far away, or looking through the internet, is not about how much blessing is given. It is based on how much I can receive, how much my mind is prepared.

Of course, there is a difference between an ordinary teacher and Buddha, but when we talk about how the Buddhas work for the benefit of beings, there is an example given. The example is of the moon in the sky. If one person takes a bowl of water and goes outside, he will see an image of the moon in the bowl of water. (In these times, there were no mirrors, or they were rare.) So, if one person goes outside with a bowl of water, there is one reflection of the moon. If two people go outside with a bowl of water, there are two reflections. If one million people go outside with a bowl of water, there are one million reflections.

Even if it becomes one million or two million or a hundred million, each reflection does not become any less clear. The reflection of the moon in the bowl I carry is not dependent on how many people are getting a reflection of the moon. It depends on how clear my water is, and that I am not shaking it, and so on. It is not about the medium, it is about my own preparedness, my devotion and that kind of thing.

So, therefore, I feel that if a really great master like His Holiness the Dalai Lama is giving a teaching, it doesn't matter if he is giving it to thousands or millions of people online, or if he is giving it to a small group in a room. How much people will receive depends on themselves. That is what I think.

Feeling everything is healed

Student: From similar practices I have done in the past, like Chenrezig, I understand that it is the feeling that is important in visualisation, rather than getting the visualisation perfect itself? Is that right?

Rinpoche: Yes. Generally, it is said that, when we are talking about visualisation, it is not necessarily visual only. It is all the senses, like seeing and hearing and feeling, altogether. Most important is feeling because that is where our main experience is. But there are also different kinds of people. Some people can easily see things in their mind. Some people can easily hear things in their mind. And some people can easily feel. Different kinds of people can start with what is more natural to them. That is the general understanding.

If you are more of a visual person, then you can use seeing. But if you are more of a feeling or a hearing type of person, then you can use that, because it is actually the same. It is actually a training, a training to have that kind of an experience. The main thing is having the experience of a more enlightened experience.

Student: So, can I ask, if the feeling is more important, about when you were explaining the sadhana and you said, 'Feel as if everything is already purified, everything is already healed, have this kind of a sense.' What I find is that my scepticism, my doubt, jumps in and says, 'Yeah, I don't believe it is though.' Does that matter? Does that matter if that feeling is there?

Rinpoche: It's true, we all know that it is not all healed! But we keep on doing the practice like this again and again. The idea is that if we are feeling, 'There is *so* much to be healed and *so* much to purify, it is impossible to heal everybody and purify everything,' then at that moment we are feeling that negative thing within us. But if you can somehow feel, even a little bit, that everything is healed and everybody is okay, then you would have to feel okay yourself. Suppose you are in a room and you feel that everybody in that room is your friend, then how would you feel?

Student: Very good.

Rinpoche: Very relaxed, very happy, yes? But if you feel that there are many people in the room who are not your friends, then you would not feel so relaxed or so good, would you? You never know, maybe they are not all exactly your friends, but how you see things makes all the difference. So, it is not useful to feel that everybody is against you, because that actually harms you more. It is a little bit like this kind of an attitude that we are using in the practice.

Eventually, however, if you look a little bit deeply, actually everybody has Buddhanature. So, fundamentally, there is nothing really wrong there with anybody. They think they are wrong, because they react in a wrong way. We all have negative feelings and negative things, not because we are totally bad or because we are something totally wrong. It is because there is something wrong with the way we perceive. So, in a deep way, it is not completely untrue, what we try and feel in the practice.

A training of discovering yourself

Student: I want to ask about my experience in two places: one is on the cushion, in formal meditation, and the other is when I am in daily life, going to work, at home etc. What happens to me is that I might start a Deity practice, and I feel I am the Deity, more or less, sometimes very strongly – which I understand is called 'Vajra Pride.' But then I get distracted and I lose it. I was hoping you could give me some tips or advice, first of all for when I am practising on the cushion, when I lose that feeling, but then also, secondly, how to bring it into daily life?

Rinpoche: All these practices, whether they are visualisations or simple meditation on the breath or meditating on loving-kindness and compassion, all of these need to be seen as a training. You have to understand the main reason you are doing it. For instance, when you visualise Tara, it is not that you become somebody different. It is not that you become somebody which you are not. That would be very fake.

Rather, it is about having a certain understanding, about the way your consciousness is. It has its clarity, which is emptiness, but there is always continual radiance, with all kinds of manifestations possible from that. These manifestations can be samsaric manifestations. These manifestations can be enlightened manifestations. It depends on where you are. The way you are when you are enlightened, and when you are not enlightened, are exactly the same. But when you are not enlightened, then you are reacting with those negative manifestations or displays. And when you are enlightened, those same manifestations, you see as enlightened manifestation. It is all about the view, the perspective.

So, therefore, what we need to train on, is transforming those samsaric manifestations into enlightened manifestations. And we use the medium of someone like Tara, or whoever, someone enlightened, to train in that. If you understand this, then the visualisation of that becomes, not a fake thing, but a training of discovering yourself. That is the first thing.

Secondly, when you do this visualisation, you try to remain in that state of positive feeling, wisdom, kindness, purity and so forth, for some time. Then, when you come out of that and go about your daily life, that is actually the main time that counts; when you are not meditating, when you are not on your cushion. The time you practise on your cushion is just an exercise. The real practice is when you are not on your cushion. Sometimes that is called 'post-meditation,' but it is the real life. The practice that you do on your cushion needs, therefore, to affect how you react, how you do things and how you carry yourself, in your daily life.

Post-meditation is the real practice. And there you should be able to connect, even a little bit, with the practice you do on your cushion. Remaining a little bit mindful of what is going on, what you are doing, with your body, speech and mind. Or wishing well to others, remembering to send a little bit of healing light from your heart if you see someone in a difficult situation. Or remembering Tara and sending a little bit of blessing to someone. When this happens, then your life becomes very much affected by your practice. Eventually so much so, that even in your dreams, you can act like this. Then you know your practice has gone deeper into yourself. And this is the important thing.

We can use the Deity practice to remember in our everyday life that, in essence, the way we are is nothing negative. We can feel kindness, compassion and wisdom; we can do that. If you can feel, when you are visualising Tara, a kind of radiance of loving-kindness and compassion, then the real test is: Can you feel a little bit of that in your everyday life, even when you are not meditating on visualising Tara?

Essence of the practice

Student: I find it very hard to visualise Tara during practice, with all the details and everything, it just doesn't come naturally. Can you give me some pointers about where to start?

Rinpoche: The main thing during the practice is feeling some kind of radiating loving-kindness and compassion. And that is enough. So, you can feel that sometimes, and sometimes you can recite the mantra and just listen to the sound of it. It doesn't need to be very complicated. I think it's important not to complicate things. The main thing is what we are training. Of course, we are training at a few different levels, but the main thing we are training with this meditation is the mind to become calm and clear. So, if you just listen to the mantra and hear that, while you are saying it, and just relax in that, not making anything more complicated out of it; at that time, you cannot think or feel or see in your mind all the problems and difficulties and complicated things. So, therefore, your mind becomes calm, your mind becomes clear and you become much more relaxed.

If you can do that for five minutes, that's a very good practice. And if you can get the knack of that a little bit, just relaxing in that, then you can do it any time your mind is a little bit distracted. Any time your mind is disturbed or having problems, you can just go into that way of being. And then you get this confidence that, 'Yes, I have a way. I don't need to be disturbed and caught up in problems all the time.

Whenever I am disturbed and troubled, I can just drop that, and go into a certain kind of meditation, whether that is listening to a sound, or thinking about a form, or just breathing.

I think this kind of training is the important thing. When you develop the ability that you can do this at any time if you wish to, that brings a great confidence. You have then found a way to be okay even when you are troubled or disturbed. You can start by doing this when everything is okay and you are fine, so you can do it in a leisurely way. But then you can develop it so you can do it when you are in trouble, when you have difficult emotions, or things are going wrong, or you are not well. If you are able to do it, even a little bit, under these circumstances, then you really have some practice, because that is much more difficult. And then, if you can do it when you are dying, then you have got it!

Our reality

Student: Is our daily perception that we usually have, compared to our visualisation of Tara, are they *as real* as each other? My other question is whether this kind of deity practice can 'bypass' our karma? Because I consider how we see things at present to be a result of our past karma, so if we train to see things as we do in our visualisation of Tara, does that give us a method to bypass our present karma?

Rinpoche: I think we are, in a way, trying to create a new karma. Because creating new karma is nothing more than creating a new, stronger habitual tendency. The way we are now and the way we experience things is because of all the things that we have done, or all the habitual tendencies that we have accumulated, so far. Now, maybe we want to change that. We could change it for better, or for worse. If we want to change it for the better, we have to do something that will help us feel more kindness, more compassion, more purity, more wisdom, and things like that. This practice is a training to do that. So, yes, it is trying to change our habitual tendencies, which you could also call our karma.

Student: So, is the visualisation we create, in the end, as real as the perception we have of the world now, just normally?

Rinpoche: How real it feels depends on how good we are at visualising, how strongly we can create that. It is based on the understanding that how we experience the world around us is not just because of how things are, but also because of how *we are*. So, therefore, if I transform, everything around me is also transformed. And if I want to transform the environment around me, I have to transform myself – the way I see, the way I hear, the way I experience. So that is why we use these kind of methods.

But, when we do the visualisations, we say that – ideally - it should be clear, and as clear as we experience things right now, but it should not be solid. It should be more like a rainbow, not too solid.

Clarity, enlightenment and samsara

Student: My question is a little bit like the last one. When you were talking about the nature of enlightenment you were saying how it is basically about how we perceive things. And I was wondering if, in the enlightened state, you see the samsaric world, but you literally see it differently; or if it is that you see the samsaric world and you are not triggered by it in the same way, so it appears different? I'm interested in how negativity is seen from an enlightened perspective - whether you see it at all, or you see through it, or it doesn't exist?

Rinpoche: I will say what they say about Buddha, because you cannot be more enlightened than the Buddha. They say Buddha can see all the realms, as they are experienced themselves. But, at the same time, Buddha can also see that the way they appear is not completely true or truly existing like that. He can also see what has happened in the past, what will happen in the future, and across all time and space. Yet, he also sees that everything is also completely pure.

Student: So, there is nothing negative, there is nothing samsaric?

Rinpoche: No, no, there is samsara, but when you understand the way things really are, you see that samsara is just a perception. Samsara cannot actually exist on its own. But there is perception of samsara. Just as there is perception of heaven or perception of 'free from samsara.' But there is nothing there called 'free from samsara' existing on its own, either.

Student: So, it really is all about our own perception and the transformation of our own perception?

Rinpoche: Yes, and within that anything can happen. Usually they explain it like this: our mind has three qualities. One is what we call emptiness; there is nothing we can hold onto. There is nothing we can hold onto and say, 'This is the mind, this is consciousness.' But at the same time, there is this clarity. There is a knowing quality, and it is clear, and everything is there. The third quality is that anything can manifest out of that.

So, the mind is a little bit like space. Can you say space is there? You cannot say space is actually there because there is nothing there, in the space, because space is actually empty. But without the space, you cannot have all the things, like stars and whole universes; but they are there. Universes are there, and lights are there, and all kinds of things are there. And they are there because of the space. Because there is the space, all the stars are shining. But space does not say, 'These are my stars,' or 'I don't want the stars to be like that.' Everything just appears. All different kinds of things appear in the space, good things, bad things, nice things, not so nice things – but 'nice' or 'not so nice' just arises according to the person.

The awareness or clarity, we make it into an identity - 'me' - and so there is an 'I.' But actually, there is no thing called 'me,' there is just this clarity. We mistake the clarity as 'me.'

Student: You said it so simply before and I thought, what a huge mistake: we impute the 'I' on this empty awareness, and then everything follows from that.

Rinpoche: And that is what we call basic ignorance.

Emanations of White Tara

Student: You said that Tara herself vowed to only come in female form, but I've heard of male teachers who are said to be emanations of Tara, or White Tara. For example, I heard Garchen Rinpoche was an emanation of White Tara. I've never understood how that works.

Rinpoche: I don't know, but there should not be restrictions concerning emanations. Enlightened Beings can emanate, not only as male and female forms, but also as objects or anything really. Then, also, all of us have a feminine side in us, as well as a masculine side.

Post-meditation practice

Student: When you were talking about taking the White Tara practice into everyday life, the post-meditation practice being the important bit. What form would that practice take in your mind if you came across someone who was suffering in your life, for example? What shape would an immediate Tara practice take in that moment?

Rinpoche: If you meet someone who is suffering, and you want to use your White Tara practice to help that person, you can do the same as during the practice in that you can visualise yourself as White Tara or you can visualise White Tara on top of your head and then in your mind you can send healing lights to that person. Even just on the spot.

Student: Also, towards yourself if you're having a particularly hard time?

Rinpoche: Yes, the same thing.

Green Tara and White Tara

Student: What is the difference between practising Green Tara and White Tara? I can see Green Tara and White Tara look different, for example, Green Tara doesn't have the seven eyes; but I would like to know what the difference is, in the result, of practising each?

Rinpoche: I think usually there is not very much difference, one is green, and one is white, and there are many different types of Tara altogether. All of them are great Bodhisattvas, Enlightened Beings, and emanations of the one being in a way. There are slightly different energies, you could say. White Tara is particularly for healing and the longevity of life, eliminating illness and developing wisdom and positive qualities. Green Tara is supposed to be more for activities, to get all the positive activities accomplished quickly. But generally, they are the same. You can actually do the same kind of sadhana, in the same way, but instead of visualising yourself as White Tara, you can visualise yourself as Green Tara, and then say the mantra. Or you can keep doing White Tara and then turn to Green Tara, also.

Conclusion

Healing

There are two things, the Relative Truth and the Ultimate Truth. Ultimately, everything is illusory and everything is a little bit like a dream. Nothing has real substance; nothing truly exists on its own; and therefore, everything is relative. But that does not mean that what you dream is not important. It is better to have good dreams than bad dreams. It is sometimes nicer to have a very good dream, rather than a horrible dream. Therefore, we have to be not too attached or solidifying things. 'I want to be healed; I want to be healed.' Too much of that makes it 'not healed.' Too much 'I want to be happy,' is itself unhappiness, because you are kind of holding on to unhappiness and *wanting* to be happy. So, therefore, wanting to be happy, to be healed, to be well, that itself is the problem, in one way.

Of course, we want to be happy and healed. This may sound a little bit contradictory, when people say you should not expect results, you should not look forward to any result. But if we don't look forward towards any results, we would not do anything. So, it is not possible to have completely no wishes for any result.

But it is also a fact that if I want something too much, that then is the problem or the main obstacle to that. So, therefore, we need to learn to look at it in a particular way. If I say 'one taste' I don't know if that will give the meaning. We need to relax and let things be. Desiring something too much is not useful. If you want to be in peace, you can't grasp at peace, because you will then be intensely disturbing yourself, instead. Maybe you just have to shut your door, maybe your windows too.

We have to learn how to take things without too much grasping. The real peace comes when you allow it to come, not wishing for it and struggling to get it. This is something we have to understand and use it like that. Sometimes, the best healing is to accept illness. If I have to die, the best way is to accept it: 'If I have to die now, let me die, no problem.' Then, sometimes you can have a very strong sense of relief, because you are ready and prepared and okay, so the anxiety of dying and changing is released and you can feel much more peaceful. When we are peaceful and ready to face anything, we are calm. And in that state, it is much easier to heal.

From the Buddhist point of view, there are always many different causes and conditions for everything, and it is the same for healing. There are many different causes and conditions that come together for healing to happen. One is that our mind is pure; the less disturbance we have in our mind, the stronger the healing. The more clear our mind is, the more focused we can be with our mind, the greater the power of healing. The more positive deeds we accumulate also increases the power of healing. When our mind is in a very positive state, especially if we have some wisdom and can allow our mind to be more clear and see the natural state of our mind, there is greater power of healing. If our mind has more confidence, more devotion, more trust, that also increases the power of healing.

The strength of dedication is also a factor; the more compassion with which we practise, the stronger and wider the aspiration we make, the stronger the healing. So, therefore, it is not only the meditation that we do that matters. But also, how we are and how we live, the whole thing together. It is said that the more we are able to advance in our own transformation, in purifying our own state of mind, the greater the healing we are able to offer others.

For this reason, sometimes practitioners do a lot of practice, like this White Tara practice, on retreat and so forth, before they offer healing to others. There are different minimum amounts of practice it is possible to observe for this. For example, some people might practise for a certain length of time, like undertaking a six-month retreat, or sometimes a three-month retreat. Some people do a certain number of recitations of a mantra, like one million recitations of the short Tara mantra would be a traditional number. And some people practise until they receive some kind of a sign of accomplishment, which could be an actual happening, or sometimes a dream. These are the three traditional measures but it is not necessary to worry about them too much.

Healing is a definite possibility. Whether we can do it, or how we can do it, is another matter. One of the main factors in this, is our state of mind. The more calm we are, the more we can deal with our emotions, the more our mind is in harmony and undisturbable, the better. There are also certain yogas and pranayamas and things like that, for this. Of course, there are also medicines. And how we live is very important; how we eat, how we sleep, and so forth. I am told, which I believe very much to be true, that you should never miss your breakfast. How we eat also has a big connection with our state of mind.

Healing in this practice is mainly happening, then, during the mantra recitation, receiving the essence of the Five Elements, and the blessings of all the worldly and enlightened great beings. Firstly, for yourself and then for all others.

Living and dying well

Dharma practice is about the art of living, in a joyful positive way. And also, about how to die. These two things go together. Because if you don't have a certain kind of confidence about how to deal with your death, you cannot live fully happily. Because your death is definitely going to happen. Everybody died before us and everybody continues to die eventually. But we are all afraid of dying. We don't know what is going to happen. We go somewhere or something happens that we don't know what it is. There is nothing we can carry there. So, it is something challenging for everyone. Therefore, everybody does have concern and worry about death.

If we have some kind of confidence about dealing with death, that really helps to make us truly confident and happy in life. If I can do something to change a difficult thing in life, I have no need to worry or be afraid about it, I can change it. If there is nothing I can do to change it, there is no *use* in worrying or being afraid about it. If I can deeply understand this, it is just an attitude, an understanding that what will happen will happen; when I have to face it, I will face it; there is no need to be afraid or worry because there is no use. Whatever will happen, I will do my best to make things as good as possible for the future, for now, but then, more than that, I cannot do. So, whatever will come, I will face it. This is just a simple attitude, nothing very big, but even just this helps. It is a complete acceptance. Acceptance does not mean I don't do anything. I do whatever I think is helpful and useful, I do healing or whatever I can, but then I accept whatever happens, happens.

And then I accept that everything is impermanent. Everybody dies. There is no certainty as to when. So, therefore, even if I die tonight, it should be okay, I can accept that. The more you are prepared, the less fear there is. When you are really able to face the reality, then the fear is much less. You have a different attitude. If you are prepared for death, then you are prepared for anything, and when you are prepared for anything, you can lead a more joyful life. There are always good things and bad things in life. Life is about facing and working with difficult situations.

This is the important thing: how to face life's problems. If you really understand the ultimate nature of things, then you understand that there is nothing called death. Because everything is changing momentarily. So, therefore, everything is dying and being born, momentarily. Every day, things are changing; every hour and every moment, things are changing; every year, things are changing. And then, if you look really closely, what is it that is changing? My body is not really even me, and it is changing all the time. My mind, what is there? It is something which doesn't have any substance; it cannot be cut into two pieces. So, therefore, it cannot be destroyed. Once we really understand the nature of things, in this way, we transcend death. There is nothing to be anxious about or protect ourselves from. The only thing left is how to help others, so compassion and wisdom are together.

In deity or Yidam practice, we allow our mind to dissolve or merge into the compassionate wisdom being. You can also do this at the time of death. This is one type of Phowa. Your identity dissolves into that and so you don't need to defend or worry about your continuation. This may not be so easy to understand but it is one way of facing death. Once we are prepared for death, we can live our life well. We should live every moment as joyfully, as purposefully, as compassionately, as possible. Then we will have lived our life well. It does not matter how long our life is. We always want to live long but we don't want to get old. But these two must go together.

We should do everything possible to cure our body of any disease and we should make ourselves healthier. And we should live as happily, and as healthily, and as well, as possible. But if we are not going to live that long, it is okay. It is not about how long we live. Sometimes it helps people to realise this. Everybody is dying, we are all dying and we don't know when we will die. No one does. There is a saying: 'During the lifetime of a terminally ill person, thousands of completely healthy people die.' So, we need to be prepared to die at any time. And then, when we die, we die. That understanding and acceptance should allow us to focus more on what is important: what we do now, today.

The origin of Tara practice

Tara practice originally came from India. The Tara tantra is sometimes called the mother of all tantras. It was the first of the tantra practices taught by the Buddha. Sometimes people think that tantra practice started before Buddhism, but now it seems that actually tantra practice first began in Buddhism and then went to Hinduism. Tara tantras are some of the earliest tantra practices and Tara practice was very popular in India. It was commonly done during the time of Nalanda University and people did this practice very publicly.

Atisha Dipamkara did this practice a lot; he was a very devoted Tara practitioner. He had a strong connection with Tara and said that she guided him and saved him many times. There are many stories about that. He was invited to Tibet in order to rekindle pure Buddhist practice in Tibet. He was invited by a descendent of the king of Tibet. At that time Tibet was divided and split into many regions. There was corruption and Buddhism was not thriving. This uncle and his nephew wanted to bring a great Indian master to Tibet to revive Buddhism and they were trying to gather the funds for that. But, meanwhile, the uncle was kidnapped by a Muslim lord from the Kashmir region, who demanded a lot of gold for his ransom. They demanded as much gold as the weight of his body. But his nephew only had enough gold for the weight of the uncle's body without his head. They were trying to get more gold but the uncle wrote secretly and asked them not to give their gold for this purpose, but to use it to bring a great Indian master to Tibet, because this was his ultimate wish and ambition.

So, his nephew followed his wishes and that is why he sent people to find the greatest Buddhist master in India at that time. They found out that Atisha Dipamkara was the most learned and most respected and most accomplished Buddhist master in India at that time. They sent an invitation to him to come to Tibet to teach and they also arranged translators and everything. At that time, Atisha was already a little aged, and everybody around him advised him not to go to Tibet. They said the people were complete barbarians and would never understand Buddhism, that he would be wasting his time. They said it would be the worst thing for himself too, he would not be able to breathe in the high altitude and so on. So, he went anyway. And the reason he went was because he went to Bodhgaya and prayed in front of a statue of Tara and asked for some kind of indication of whether he should go to Tibet or not. And then, it is said that the Tara spoke and said that, if he went to Tibet it would be very useful and very beneficial for Tibet, but that he would never come back, he would die there. So, he went.

Tara was one of his main practices and this practice actually comes from him. He did not teach much Vajrayana but he did teach Tara practice. And then, from there, through a few generations, came Gampopa and then the first Karmapa. So, the lineage is something that has been practised over more than a thousand years in Tibet. And it is regarded as a very auspicious and effective practice; a practice that has been tested by time. It is good for your own transformation and for healing, clearing obstacles and for helping other people, also.

All Vajrayana practices are in many ways the same, and this is what I was trying to explain. Sometimes these kind of practices are mistaken as mainly a traditional ritual, something that is very culturally-influenced and Tibetan. If you practise these in a Tibetan monastic environment, then of course they are done in a very traditional way, in a very Tibetan way; and they can be a tradition, a ritual. But the real practice is not about tradition and ritual, and is not culturally-bound. It is a training, a practice. And so, the important part is to see where the training is, to see where the practice is. If we understand what it is training and practising on, and we can connect with that, then the whole thing becomes a Dharma practice. It becomes a training to transform yourself and teaches you to develop techniques to heal yourself, and heal others. Then, it is nothing to do with Tibetan ritual tradition, and that is how it should be. But we have to understand it, in order for it to be like that.

ༀ་ཏུ་རེ་ཏུཏྟ་རེ་ཏུ་རེ་སྭཱ་ཧཱ།

A Short Daily Practice for White Tara

by Tenga Rinpoche

with translation based on a commentary by Ringu Tulku Rinpoche

TAM

DHRUM   PAM   A

OM   AH   HUNG

ན་མོ།
Namo
སངས་རྒྱས་ཆོས་དང་དགེ་འདུན་ལ། །
sang gyä chö dang gen dün la
སྒོ་གསུམ་གུས་པས་སྐྱབས་སུ་མཆི། །
go sum gü pay kyab su chi
མཁའ་མཉམ་སེམས་ཅན་ཐམས་ཅད་ཀུན། །
kha nyam sem chen tham che kün
སངས་རྒྱས་ཐོབ་ཕྱིར་སེམས་བསྐྱེད་དོ། །
sang gyä thob chir sem kye do

Namo,
With deep reverence and humility of body, speech and mind,
I take refuge in Buddha, Dharma and Sangha.
And I generate bodhicitta so that all beings, as limitless as space,
May attain perfect Buddhahood.

(Repeat three times)

ཨོཾ་ཤུ་ཉ་ཏཱ་ཛྙཱ་ན་བཛྲ་སྭ་བྷཱ་ཝ་ཨཱཏྨ་ཀོ྅ཧཾ།
OM SHUNYATA JNANA BENZA SOBHAVA ETMAKO HAM

A Short Daily Practice for White Tara

སྟོང་པའི་དང་ལས་ཧཱུྃ་སྒྲས་སྲུང་འཁོར་དཀར། །
tong pä ngang lä hung drä sung khor kar

དེ་དབུས་དྷྲུཾ་ལས་ཆུ་ཤེལ་གཞལ་ཡས་ཁང་། །
de ü dhrum lä chu shel shäl yä khang

དབུས་སུ་པཾ་ལས་པདྨ་ཨ་ལས་ཟླ། །
ü su pam lä pema a lä da

རང་སེམས་ཏཾ་དཀར་ཡོངས་གྱུར་ཨུཏྤལ། །
rang sem tam kar yong gyur utpala

ཏཾ་གྱིས་མཚན་ལས་འོད་འཕྲོས་དོན་གཉིས་བྱས། །
tam gyi tsen lä ö thrö dön nyi jä

ཡོངས་གྱུར་རང་ཉིད་ཡིད་བཞིན་འཁོར་ལོ་ནི། །
yong gyur rang nyi yi shin khor lo ni

ཆུ་ཤེལ་ལྟར་དཀར་ཞལ་གཅིག་ཕྱག་གཉིས་པ། །
chu shel tar kar shäl chig chag nyi pa

གཡས་པས་མཆོག་སྦྱིན་གཡོན་པས་ཨུཏྤལ་འཛིན། །
yä pä chog jin yön pä utpal dzin

ཞབས་གཉིས་སྐྱིལ་ཀྲུང་རིན་ཆེན་རྒྱན་གྱིས་སྤྲས། །
shap nyi kyil trung rin chen gyen gyi trä

དར་གྱི་ཤམ་ཐབས་ཟླ་བར་རྒྱབ་བརྟེན་པའི། །
dar gyi sham thab da war gyab ten pä

Out of emptiness, by the power of the sound of HUNG, appears a white protection circle, like a huge tent.
In its centre, from the syllable DHRUM, appears a palace of white crystal.
In the centre of the palace, appears a PAM, which becomes a thousand-petalled lotus flower, with an A upon it.
The A transforms into a moon disc, and on this moon disc, my own mind appears as a white TAM, which then transforms into an utpala flower, with my mind as TAM in its centre.

The TAM radiates light, bringing in the blessings of Tara and all the Enlightened Beings.
The light radiates a second time, transforming, healing and purifying all the beings of the Six Realms.
In this way, the two purposes are accomplished.
The light dissolves back into the TAM, instantly transforming me into White Tara, the Wish-Fulfilling Wheel.

White, like crystal, with one face and two hands,
Adorned with precious jewels and a lower garment of silk,
Her right hand is in the mudra of supreme giving, the left holds an utpala flower.
Her legs are in vajra posture; her back is supported by a moon disc.

གནས་གསུམ་འབྲུ་གསུམ་ཐུགས་དབུས་པད་ཟླར་ཏཱཾ། །
nä sum dru sum thug ü pe da tam

དེ་ལས་འོད་འཕྲོས་ཡེ་ཤེས་སྤྱན་དྲངས་བསྟིམ། །
de lä o thrö ye she chen drang tim

In the three places, are the three syllables OM AH HUNG.
In the heart centre, on a lotus and a moon disc, is the white TAM.
Light radiates and invites the Jnanasattva, which dissolves into myself.

སླར་ཡང་འོད་འཕྲོས་དབང་ལྷ་སྤྱན་དྲངས་ཏེ། །
lar yang ö thrö wang lha chen drang te

དབང་བསྐུར་སྐུ་གང་རིགས་བདག་སྣང་མཐའ་གསལ། །
wang kur ku gang rig dag nang tha säl

Again, light radiates, inviting all the Empowerment Deities.
They grant empowerment and amrita fills my body.
The overflow at the crown of my head appears as Amitabha, Buddha of Boundless Light.

ཐུགས་དབུས་པད་ཟླར་འཁོར་ལོ་རྩིབ་བརྒྱད་སྟེར། །
thug ü pe dar khor lo tsib gye ter

སྟེང་འོག་ཨོཾ་ཧཱུྃ་དབུས་སུ་ཏཾ་ཡིག་དཀར། །
teng og om ha ü su tam yig kar

མུ་ཁྱུད་ནང་མར་སྔགས་ཀྱི་ཕྲེང་བ་དང་། །
mu khyü nang mar ngag kyi threng wa dang

རྩིབ་བརྒྱད་སྟེང་དུ་ཡི་གེ་བརྒྱད་བཅས་གསལ། །
tsib gye teng du yi ge gye chä säl

དེ་ལས་འོད་འཕྲོས་འབྱུང་ལྔའི་དྭངས་མ་བསྡུས། །
de lä ö thrö jung ngä dang ma dü

སླར་ཡང་འོད་འཕྲོས་ལྷ་དང་དྲང་སྲོང་དང་། །
lar yang ö thrö lha dang drang song dang

རིག་འཛིན་རྣམས་ཀྱི་ཚེ་ཡི་དངོས་གྲུབ་བསྡུས། །
rig dzin nam kyi tse yi ngö drub dü

སླར་འཕྲོས་སངས་རྒྱས་བྱང་སེམས་བྱིན་རླབས་དང་། །
lar thrö sang gyä jang sem jin lab dang

ཚེ་ཡི་དངོས་གྲུབ་བསྡུས་ནས་ཏཾ་ལ་ཐིམ། །
tse yi ngö drub dü nä tam la thim

འཆི་མེད་ཚེ་ཡི་དངོས་གྲུབ་ཐོབ་པར་གྱུར། །
chi me tse yi ngö drub thob par gyur

In the heart centre, on the lotus and moon disc,
Is a hollow white wheel with eight spokes.
In the centre of the wheel is the seed syllable TAM, with OM above and HA below.
Around the inner circle of the wheel, stands the mantra garland, radiating light.

The light radiates through the vastness of space, gathering the pure essences of all the Five Elements, which dissolve into myself.
Again, light radiates, collecting the blessings and long-life siddhis of all the enlightened and worldly deities, gods, Vidyadharas and rishis who have accomplished long-life practice.
Light radiates a third time, inviting the completely enlightened blessings and siddhis of all the Buddhas and Bodhisattvas to dissolve into the TAM.
Thus, the siddhi of deathless life is accomplished.

ཨོཾ་ཏཱ་རེ་ཏུཏྟཱ་རེ་ཏུ་རེ་སྭཱ་ཧཱ།

OM TARE TUTTARE TURE SOHA

ཨོཾ་ཏཱ་རེ་ཏུཏྟཱ་རེ་ཏུ་རེ་མ་མ་ཨཱ་ཡུཿ་པུཎྱེ་ཛྙཱ་ན་པུཥྚིཾ་ཀུ་རུ་སྭཱ་ཧཱ།

OM TARE TUTTARE TURE MAMA AYUH PUNYE JNANA PUKTIM KURU SOHA

སྣོད་བཅུད་འོད་ཞུ་སྲུང་འཁོར་གཞལ་ཡས་ཁང་། །
nö chü ö shu sung khor shäl yä khang
རང་ལ་ཐིམ་ཞིང་རང་ཡང་ཏཾ་ལ་ཐིམ། །
rang la thim shing rang yang tam la thim
ཏཾ་ཡང་འོད་ཞུ་མ་བཅོས་གཉུག་མའི་དང་། །
tam yang ö shu ma chö nyug mä ngang
རང་བབ་སོ་མའི་ཀློང་དུ་མཉམ་པར་བཞག །
rang bab so mä long du nyam par shag

The container and the contained, the whole universe and all beings, melt into light and dissolve into the protection circle.
The circle melts into the crystal palace and the crystal palace melts into myself as White Tara.
Tara dissolves into the seed syllable TAM and the TAM itself slowly dissolves, from the bottom of the lotus flower to the tip of the nadi, and melts into light.
I allow my mind to rest in its original purity,
And remain, freshly settled, in the uncontrived, natural space.

སླར་ཡང་རྗེ་བཙུན་འཕགས་མའི་སྐུ་རུ་ལྡང་། །
lar yang je tsün phag mä ku ru dang
དགེ་བས་སེམས་ཅན་སངས་རྒྱས་ཐོབ་པར་ཤོག །
ge wä sem chen sang gyä thob par shog

Once again, I arise in the form of Noble Tara.
Through this merit, may all sentient beings attain Buddhahood.

སརྦ་མངྒལོ་ཛཱ་ཡནྟུ།། །།

Sarva Mangalam Dzayantu
All is auspicious. May there be victory!

His Eminence Benchen Tulku Tenga Rinpoche composed this concise daily practice text. This English translation was put together by the Bodhicharya team, based on a line-by-line verbal translation and commentary by Ringu Tulku Rinpoche.

As Ringu Tulku explains earlier, the Tibetan, or English, or both, can be recited. (If only English is recited, the mantras are included with the English.)

———— denotes places it is possible to pause, to deepen meditation and/or clarify the visualisation.

Six Protection Lights

The Six Lights practice can be included during the mantra recitation. It works particularly on our emotions; the five emotions and the five wisdoms. First we feel that, from the *TAM* inside our heart centre, a white light radiates and this white light fills our whole body and we feel that all illnesses, obstacles, obscurations, negative karma, and all negative things, are purified. We feel totally purified. Then the light radiates beyond our body and it touches all the people beyond us, in this town, in this country, in this continent, in the whole world; and whoever is touched by this light is healed and purified. The whole world becomes purified, peaceful, and joyful; all peaceful activities are accomplished.

After radiating, the light remains, forming a further protection tent or sphere of white light, beyond the protection tent that we visualised originally. So, it remains, continuing to provide that power of purification. It is like a rainbow; you see it in a very spacious way. The space between the protection tent and the layer of white light is filled with freshly-opening, dewy, utpala flowers.

Secondly, a radiance of yellow light radiates from the *TAM,* golden yellow like polished gold. This fills your body and increases your lifespan. Yellow is the colour or energy of increasing, developing, progressing, and enriching. So, you feel that it brings you long lifespan, good fortune, prosperity, wealth, good position, fame, everything you need, including meditation experiences and realisation. Then yellow light rays radiate outwards transforming the whole world in this way, bringing long life and prosperity and good position to everybody. All activities of increasing are accomplished. The light remains after, as another layer of light beyond the white light. And between the layers of light, there is space and, again, flowers bloom.

Then we apply the same procedure for the four other lights. Third is red light, the colour of rubies, and it brings power or empowerment. It also represents wisdom, love, power, and positive energy. It brings all that to you, and then to the whole world. The red light is absorbed and the activities of empowering are accomplished. There appears a tent of red light, in a similarly spacious way, beyond the yellow.

Then blue light radiates, and this light destroys all that is negative or adverse, such as the five poisons, enemies, those that mis-guide; anything that is harmful or creates problems and difficulties, is cleared. All wrathful activity is thus accomplished because this blue light is destructive, destroying negative forces. It does the same for the whole world and then remains as a tent of blue light around the red light.

Then green light, the colour of emeralds, radiates in the same way. This light accomplishes all activities that need to happen. All your positive wishes and desires and projects to bring benefit to yourself and others, all these are accomplished. For yourself, and then radiating throughout the world, and remaining as a layer of green light beyond the blue.

Finally, purple or violet light radiates; the colour is taught as 'blue mixed with dark red.' The other five colours we have visualised so far are used in many practices, for example for transforming the five emotions into the five wisdoms, and corresponding to the five Buddha families. But we don't find this colour used in other practices; this is special for White Tara practice. This colour is to make things stable. When you are healing, that healing has to be stabilised.

The purple light radiates and is absorbed, first by yourself and then throughout the world, stabilising the healing which has been accomplished, so it cannot be destroyed. Everything accomplished so far remains undisturbed and cannot be shaken. As each time, a layer of light remains outside the previous layer, and flowers bloom between the layers.

> White light – purifying
> Yellow light – increasing
> Red light – empowering
> Blue light – clearing obstacles
> Green light – accomplishing activities
> Purple light – stabilising

The spheres of light remain around the initial protection tent we visualised; in the order we visualise them. They form an enormous protection tent; big, spacious, widely-encompassing, as if surrounding the whole world. Although made of light, each layer is utterly impenetrable. This practice is sometimes called the Six Light Rays, and also the Protection Tent, or the Six Protection Lights. And in between you allow your mind to relax in its natural state.

Then, the third visualisation you can use during mantra recitation, if you want to, is Amitabha on the crown of your head. Amitabha transforms into Amitayus, Buddha of Long Life; who is the same as Amitabha (Buddha of Boundless Light) except he is wearing different clothes and holds a special vase instead of a begging bowl. You visualise that he gathers all the qualities of long life, positive energy, blessings, and wisdom, which come from all over and from the essence of the Five Elements and so forth, and these all go into him and then overflow from the vase he is holding; and fill you and all beings.

One way of doing it is to use the main Tara mantra for the first part, which is described in the text, and the longer White Tara mantra for the Six Lights and Amitayus. At the beginning, it is better to concentrate on the first part and bring these second and third parts of the practice in later. Then, if you do these, the six layers of light remain in place during the Amitayus visualisation. And everything dissolves during the dissolution: the universe dissolves into the protection lights, the Six Protection Lights dissolve, one into another, and then into the protection tent; the protection tent dissolves into the palace, the palace into Tara, and Tara into the *TAM*.

Dedication

All my babbling,
In the name of Dharma
Has been set down faithfully
By my dear students of pure vision.

I pray that at least a fraction of the wisdom
Of those enlightened teachers
Who tirelessly trained me
Shines through this mass of incoherence.

May the sincere efforts of all those
Who have worked tirelessly
Result in spreading the true meaning of Dharma
To all who are inspired to know.

May this help dispel the darkness of ignorance
In the minds of all living beings
And lead them to complete realisation
Free from all fear.

Ringu Tulku

Glossary and Notes

Editor's Note: Wherever possible, the descriptions in this glossary include Ringu Tulku's own words, gathered from a variety of teaching sources. But, as this is not always possible, the glossary is offered as a help to the reader and not a definitive authority.

Akong Rinpoche (1940 – 2013) was recognised at the age of four, as the reincarnation of the first Akong Rinpoche, Abbot of Dolma Lhakang Monastery in Tibet. He was a doctor and teacher of Tibetan Medicine, and a Dharma teacher. In 1967, he co-founded Kagyu Samye Ling Monastery and Tibetan Centre in Scotland: the first Tibetan Buddhist centre in the West. He is also the founder of ROKPA, an international humanitarian aid organisation. He was a pioneer of new approaches to mental health care, creating Tara Rokpa Therapy and establishing Lothlorien, a therapeutic community. He is the author of three books: *Taming the Tiger* (1994); *Restoring the Balance* (2005); and *Limitless Compassion* (2010). See also: *Only the Impossible is Worth Doing: Recollections of the Supreme Life and Activity of Chöje Akong Tulku Rinpoche*. Published by Dzalendra Publishing, Rokpa Trust: 2020.

Amrita (Sanskrit; *dütsi* Tibetan) literally means the immortal; the nectar (*tsi*) that conquers the demon (*dü*) of death; symbol of wisdom.

Atisha Dipamkara (982 – 1054) (Sanskrit; *Jowo Atisha* Tibetan), was a great Indian master and scholar, and one of the main teachers at the monastic university of Vikramashila. He spent the last ten years of his life teaching in Tibet, where his followers founded the Kadampa school. His most celebrated text is the *Lamp for the Path to Enlightenment*, which he wrote for the Tibetan people, and which became the source for the *Lam Rim*, or Graduated Path, tradition, found in all schools of Tibetan Buddhism.

Attachment refers to holding on too strongly to something, clinging to it; you get too close to something you perceive as 'nice' until your relating with it takes on a 'sticky' kind of feeling.

Aversion refers to a mind quality of rejecting or pushing something away; wishing it were not there and trying to eliminate it or get away from it.

Bodhicharyavatara (Sanskrit) also known as *The Bodhisattvacharyavatara* is an 8th century Mahayana text, outlining the path of the Bodhisattva. It was composed by Shantideva, a great scholar, at the famous Nalanda Monastery in Northern India. It found wide acclaim almost immediately in India and rapidly spread. It was translated into Tibetan during the 9th century. It is the key text for anyone following the Bodhisattvayana (Mahayana) or Vajrayana path. There are many translations into English from several languages. One is *The Bodhisattva's Way of Life* translated by the Padmakara Translation Group from Tibetan, revised edition: Shambhala 2006.

Bodhicitta (*Bodhichitta* Sanskrit; *chang chub kyi sem* Tibetan) is the heart essence of the Buddha, of enlightenment. The root of the word, *Bodh*, means 'to know, to have the full understanding' and *citta* refers to the heart-mind or 'heart feeling.' In a practical sense, Bodhicitta is compassion: compassion imbued with wisdom.

Bodhisattva (Sanskrit; *changchub sempa* Tibetan) comes from the root *bodh* which means 'to know, to have the full understanding.' The term describes a being that has made a commitment to work for the benefit of others to bring them to a state of lasting peace and happiness and freedom from all suffering. A Bodhisattva does not have to be a Buddhist but can come from any spiritual tradition or none. The key thing is that they have this compassionate wish to free all beings from suffering, informed by the wisdom of knowing this freedom is possible.

Buddhanature / Buddha nature (*Sugatagarba* Sanskrit; *desheg nyingpo* Tibetan) refers to the fundamental, true nature of all beings, free from all obscurations and distortions. Ultimately, our true nature, and the true nature of all beings, is inseparable from the nature of Buddha. It is the 'primordial goodness' of sentient beings, an innate all-pervasive primordial purity.

Buddha Shakyamuni, the historical Buddha, was born a Prince in Northeast India about 500 B.C.E. and left home to discover the causes of suffering. He gave the teachings that have come down the centuries to be called Buddhism.

Cakra / Chakra (Sanskrit) literally means 'wheel' or 'circle,' and describes a nexus or hub of energetic flow and interconnection, within the subtle body. As such, cakras lie at the core of our being. They can be visualised in the centre of the body, at the relevant levels. As practitioners become more advanced, the ability to feel these energetic centres, and whether they are blocked or open, may develop naturally. Different systems use different numbers of cakras; commonly seven or five or four cakras may be used. These different numbers are sometimes reached by coalescing, for example, the lower three cakras, into one cakra. As Ringu Tulku mentions in these teachings, the three main cakras used in deity yoga are at head, throat, and heart level, and represent body, speech, and mind, respectively.

Chenrezig (Tibetan; *Avalokiteshvara* Sanskrit) is the embodiment of the compassionate aspect of the mind of the Buddhas. He is revered as the patron deity of Tibet, his most common forms being the Four-armed and the Thousand-armed Chenrezig. The four arms represent the Four Immeasurables and the thousand arms represent unlimited compassionate activity throughout space and time, each hand having an eye in its palm. [Although Chenrezig is represented in male form in Tibet, Avalokiteshvara is translated as Kuan Yin in the Chinese tradition and as Kwannon in the Japanese, both represented in female form.] The mantra of Chenrezig is one of the best known: *OM MANI PEME HUNG*.

Completion Stage of Vajrayana deity practice is the genuine condition, or perfectly existent nature, that lies behind the Creation Stage. It is the natural state, characterised by great depth. So, while there may be only one or two lines in a sadhana that refer to this aspect of the practice, it is present throughout, as the backdrop or context in which the whole practice occurs. This aspect is much harder to understand and learn how to experience, than the visualisation of the Creation Stage, but it is what ultimately makes sense of the practice.

Creation / Generation Stage of Vajrayana deity practice uses our mind's innate creativity to generate an experience of positive or enlightened qualities through creating a visualisation, which is generated and then, later, dissolved.

Deity / Deities (*istadevata* Sanskrit; *yidam* Tibetan) in Buddhism, are representations of the embodiment of enlightened mind. They are visualised or depicted in various forms to bring out different aspects of that essential purity. During formal practice a deity may be visualised in front of, or above, the practitioner, or as the practitioner themselves. 'Deities encourage us to see the pure state of reality, by which we mean the state that does not bind us or create problems and is, therefore, a liberating state.'

Dharma (Sanskrit; *chö* Tibetan) The word *Dharma* has many uses. In its widest sense, it means all that can be known, or the way things are. The other main meaning is the teachings of the Buddha; also called the *Buddhadharma*. This refers to the entire body of oral and written Buddhist teachings, and includes the literal teachings and that which is learnt through practising them.

Empowerment (*abhisheka* Sanskrit; *wang* Tibetan) is a ceremony conferring the blessing and transmission of the lineage. It also serves as a teaching and an introduction to a specific practice. It is a bit like a guided meditation, that a qualified master leads students through, together invoking the blessings of the lineage and making an authentic link to that practice. To be complete, the transmission of the text (*lung*) and the explanations / instructions (*tri*) must also be received. The Empowerment, Transmission and Instruction are often referred to as the '*Wang, Lung* and *Tri*' and are an indispensable door to tantric practices.

Emptiness (*shunyata* Sanskrit; *tong pa nyi* Tibetan) The Buddha taught in the second turning of the wheel of Dharma, that all phenomena have no real, independent existence of their own. They only appear to exist as separate, nameable entities because of the way we commonly, conceptually, see things. But in themselves, all things are 'empty' of inherent existence. This includes our 'self', which we habitually unconsciously mistake to be an independently-existing, separate phenomenon. Instead, everything exists in an interdependent way and this is what the term emptiness refers to. As Ringu Tulku says in *Like Dreams and Clouds,* Bodhicharya Publications: 2011: 'Emptiness does not mean there is nothing; emptiness means the way everything is, the way everything magically manifests.'

Gampopa (1079 – 1153) was the foremost disciple of Milarepa. He was a skilled physician and family man until an epidemic took the lives of his wife and children, at which point he became a monk and dedicated his life to Dharma. He received teachings from many sources and brought together earlier streams of Kadampa and Mahamudra teaching lineages within the Kagyu school. He had many students, among them Düsum Khyenpa who became the first Karmapa. Gampopa wrote 'The Jewel Ornament of Liberation' which is now a seminal Kagyu text.

Guru Padmasambhava, also known as Guru Pema or Guru Rinpoche, can be understood in different senses. In a historical sense, he was an 8th century Indian Buddhist Master who was invited by King Trisong Detsen to re-establish Buddhism in Tibet, which included dealing with negative influences hindering this. Together with Shantarakshita, he supervised the translation of the Dharma into the Tibetan language. Padmasambhava left Tibet in 774 C.E. without having completed the full transmission of the path to enlightenment. Seeing that the times were not yet ripe, he buried further texts on Dzogchen to be unearthed and studied in later times. The Nyingma School of Tibetan Buddhism recognises him as their root guru. In another sense, Guru Rinpoche represents an archetypal or universal teacher, the guiding power that emanates from pure mind, anywhere in time and space, ultimately providing a mirror for our own innate wisdom mind.

Habitual tendencies (*She jay drib pa* Tibetan) Literally translated from Tibetan as 'obscurations of knowledge,' these refer to our propensity to act or react in certain ways, reinforced and influenced by past actions. They become ingrained in us again and again until they are habitual.

Jnanasattva (Sanskrit; *yeshe sempa* Tibetan) *Jnana* means 'wisdom' here, and *sattva* is 'being.' The Tara that we start by visualising ourselves as, is called *damzig pa* (Tibetan) or *samayasattva* (Sanskrit). And then the real, true Enlightened Beings, or Enlightened Deities, whom we invite, and who dissolve into and integrate with and become one with us, are called *yeshe sempa*, the Wisdom Beings, or Wisdom Deities; which is *Jnanasattva* in Sanskrit.

Kagyu (Tibetan) *Ka* means 'oral' and *gyu* means 'lineage:' The Lineage of Oral Transmission; also known as The Lineage of Meaning and Blessing or The Practice Lineage. It traces its origins to the primordial Buddha, Dorje Chang (Vajradhara) and the great Indian master and yogi, Tilopa. It is one of the four major schools of Tibetan Buddhism, and is headed by His Holiness the Karmapa, currently HH 17th Karmapa Ogyen Trinley Dorje. The other three main schools are the Gelug, Nyingma, and Sakya.

Karma (Sanskrit; *lay* Tibetan) literally means 'action.' It refers to the cycle of cause and effect that is set up through our actions. Actions coloured or motivated by *klesha* (see below), for example, anger or desire, will tend to create results in keeping with that action and also increase our tendency to do similar actions. These tendencies become ingrained in us and become our habitual way of being, which is our karma. According to our level of awareness, we can change our karma through consciously refining our actions.

Kleshas (Sanskrit; *nyön mong* Tibetan) are translated as mental defilements, mind poisons or negative emotions. They include any emotion or mind state that disturbs or distorts consciousness. They bring forth our experience of suffering and prevent our experience of love, joy and happiness. The three main kleshas are desire, anger and ignorance. Combinations of these give rise to the five kleshas, which are these three plus pride and envy / jealousy.

Lama (Tibetan; *guru* Sanskrit) means teacher or master. *La* refers to there being nobody higher in terms of spiritual accomplishment and *ma* refers to compassion like a mother. Thus, both wisdom and compassion are brought to fruition together in the lama. The word has the connotation of 'heavy' or 'weighty,' indicating the guru or lama is heavy with positive attributes and kindness.

Madhyamika (Sanskrit) literally means 'The Middle Way' and is the most influential of four major philosophical schools of Indian Buddhism. This Middle Way avoids falling into the extremes of either eternalism or nihilism.

Mahamudra (Sanskrit; *cha ja chen po* or *chak chen* Tibetan) literally means 'Great Seal' or 'Great Symbol,' referring to the way in which all phenomena are 'sealed' by their primordially perfect true nature. The term can denote the teaching, meditation practice or accomplishment of Mahamudra. The meditation consists in perceiving the mind directly rather than through rational analysis, and relies on a direct introduction to the nature of the essence of the mind. This form of meditation is traced back to Saraha (10th century), and was passed down in the Kagyu school through Marpa. The accomplishment lies in experiencing the non-duality of the phenomenal world and emptiness: perceiving how the two are not separate. This experience can also be called the union of emptiness and luminosity.

Mahayana (Sanskrit; *tek pa chen po* Tibetan) translates as 'Great Vehicle.' This is the second vehicle of Buddhism, and emphasises the teachings on Bodhicitta, compassion, and interdependence. It expands on the teachings of the Sravakayana (the foundational vehicle of Buddhism) and sees the purpose of enlightenment as being the liberation of *all* sentient beings from suffering, as well as oneself. This is the path of the Bodhisattva (see above) and so may also be called the Bodhisattvayana.

Mantra (Sanskrit; *ngag* Tibetan) The word mantra is an abbreviation of two syllables *mana* and *tara*, respectively meaning 'mind' and 'protection:' coming from the mind, giving protection through transformation. Mantras are Sanskrit words or syllables that express the quintessence of particular energies or of a deity. They protect the mind from distraction and serve as support for meditation. Mantras can be sung or spoken out loud, quietly recited 'just loud enough for your collar to hear' or recited silently.

Ngöndro (Tibetan) is a series of practices comprising Four Ordinary Foundations and Four Extraordinary Foundations. They were originally created for the Tibetan people by the Indian Mahasiddha, Atisha Dipamkara, and are treated as the gateway to all deep Vajrayana practices. The Ordinary Foundations are contemplations on: precious human birth, death and impermanence, karma, and samsara. The Four Extraordinary Foundations are the recitation of: 100,000 refuge prayers and prostrations, 100,000 Vajrasattva mantras, 100,000 mandala offerings, and 100,000 guru yoga practices. The Ngöndro is practised by all schools of Tibetan Buddhism with slight variations. See *The Ngöndro: Foundation Practices of Mahamudra* by Ringu Tulku, Bodhicharya Publications: 2013.

Nirvana (Sanskrit; *nyangde* Tibetan) literally means 'extinguished' and is the state of being free from all suffering. It is the opposite of samsara and arises when we have completely done away with all the obscurations, misunderstandings, negative emotions and other hindrances that create samsaric existence. When we are free from all fear and suffering and our mind is completely clear; this is described as enlightenment or nirvana.

Phowa (Tibetan) is a meditation practice of 'transferring the consciousness at the time of death.'

Rimé (Tibetan) is an ecumenical, or non-sectarian movement begun by Jamyang Khyentse Wangpo and Jamgön Kongtrul in Kham in the nineteenth century. It promotes the study of all forms of Tibetan Buddhism, without bias to any particular school. It is not a way of uniting different schools and lineages by emphasising their similarities, but is more of an appreciation of their differences and an acknowledgement of the importance of having this variety for the benefit of practitioners with different needs. It emphasizes the harmony of all paths, in accordance with the Buddha's original teaching.

Rinpoche (Tibetan) is an honorific term in the Tibetan Buddhist tradition, reserved for great masters. It refers to how precious it is that such teachers are among us; literally translating as 'precious one.'

Rishi, a highly-realised yogi or sage.

Sadhana (Sanskrit; *drub tab* Tibetan), literally 'means of accomplishment,' refers to the text of a ritual practice that may be followed by a practitioner who has been initiated into it. A typical sadhana structure usually starts with taking refuge and arousing Bodhicitta. The main part of the practice involves visualisation and mantra recitation and the sadhana concludes by dedicating the merit of the practice to all sentient beings. *See also Creation Stage and Completion Stage*.

Samsara / samsaric (Sanskrit; *khor wa* Tibetan) is the state of suffering of 'cyclical existence.' It describes a state of mind that experiences gross and / or subtle pain and dissatisfaction. It arises because the mind is deluded and unclear and thus perpetually conditioned by attachment, aversion and ignorance.

Shamatha (Sanskrit; *shiné / shinay* Tibetan) is calm abiding meditation: calming and stabilising the mind to bring it to a state of peace. Sometimes also called tranquillity meditation. *Shama* (Sanskrit) and *shi* (Tibetan) refer to 'pacification' or 'slowing or cooling down' or 'rest.' *Tha* (Sanskrit) and *né* (Tibetan) refer to 'abiding' or 'remaining.'

Siddhi is a Sanskrit noun which can be translated as 'perfection,' 'accomplishment,' 'attainment,' or 'success.' Specifically, *siddhi* describes the attainment, such as enlightenment, whereas *siddhis* refer to many types of powers, like the 'eight siddhis' and so forth.

Tantra (Sanskrit; *gyü* Tibetan) literally means 'continuity' or continuous thread (of the pure nature of mind) that runs through everything. In Buddhism, it also refers to the meditative practices of the Vajrayana, which include mantra recitation, visualisation practices, and the texts that describe these.

Tukdam is a deep meditative composure that some highly-realised masters enter into at the time of death, and remain in after their physical bodies have expired, with the body remaining fresh and without signs of decomposing, sometimes for days or even weeks.

Utpala flowers rise out of the mud and are like water lilies, or the lotus, a symbol of purity and wisdom.

Vajra (Sanskrit; *dorje* Tibetan) is sometimes translated as 'diamond-like.' It symbolises that which is indestructible, that which can cut through anything else but cannot, itself, be destroyed. The symbol is a ritual object like a kind of sceptre, made of metal. What it symbolises is the vajra state, attained through understanding the essence of mind as pure emptiness. Once this understanding is attained, we know there is nothing that can be destroyed because everything exists in emptiness. So, we realise we are indestructible in this way and this is ultimately what frees us from all fear and clinging.

Vajrayana Buddhism (Sanskrit; *dorje tek pa* Tibetan) *Vajra* means 'diamond-like' or of 'indestructible capacity,' conveying a sense of what is beyond arising and ceasing, and is therefore indestructible. The Vajrayana is the third of the three main vehicles of Buddhism and provides a path of compassionate wisdom that sees through all illusion. It incorporates and accepts all the teachings of the Sravakayana (the Foundational Vehicle) and the Bodhisattvayana (or Mahayana) and then also includes teachings on the tantras and various skilful means. It elaborates on the concept of Buddhanature and uses the method of taking the result as the path. It may afford the practitioner swift progress, practised in accordance with the foundations of Buddhist approach.

Vidyadhara (Sanskrit), literally 'wisdom-holder' or 'awareness-holder.'

Vipassana (Pali; *vipashyana* Sanskrit; *lhakthong* Tibetan) means 'Insight Meditation.' It is usually practised after gaining some experience of 'calm-abiding' meditation and refers to gaining insight into your true nature, seeing yourself truly and directly, which becomes the basis for transformation. *See also Shamatha (calm-abiding meditation)*.

Wish-Fulfilling Wheel is a name used for White Tara. It could also be translated as Wish-Fulfilling Activity or Wish-Fulfilling Accomplishment.

Yanas (Sanskrit; *tek pa* Tibetan) eg. the three yanas, the nine yanas. *Yana* means Vehicle and refers to categories of Buddhist teachings that provide approaches with different emphases. The aim of such vehicles is to provide the means of 'crossing over' to the other side: transforming life from samsaric experience to an experience of enlightenment or 'clear seeing'. The different yanas provide a different view of the journey and are suitable for different practitioners.

Yidam (Tibetan; *istadevata* Sanskrit), is literally a shortened version of the meaning 'samaya of mind.' It refers to a personification or archetype of specific enlightened qualities that a practitioner takes as their inspiration, in order to develop such qualities themselves. *See also Deity*.

Notes

- In this book, we have used the word *student* to identify questions and discussion from audience members. This is not intended to imply the speaker would necessarily identify themselves as a student of Tibetan Buddhism or of Ringu Tulku. It refers to the fact that they are being a 'student,' just in this instance, by virtue of asking a question in order to understand more.

- The English translation of Tenga Rinpoche's White Tara Sadhana presented in this book was only embarked upon subsequent to the other teachings Ringu Tulku gave, on which this book is based. Thus, this is a new translation, based on Ringu Tulku's own line by line translation and commentary. There is also an audio recording of this practice, including this translation as well as the Tibetan, provided in the Ringu Tulku Teachings Archive, on the page for the White Tara Sadhana teaching given in 2020 (https://bodhicharya.org/product/white-tara).

- In the sadhana translation: there are some places where a little more detail is given on the visualisation in the English, than is strictly present in the Tibetan. These aspects are implied by the Tibetan and were taken from Ringu Tulku's commentary and translation of the sadhana. It was felt they were helpful to include, in reciting the sadhana.

- In the sadhana translation: the lines below, referring to the Completion Stage, are very difficult to translate (since the experience pointed towards is impossible to put into words, in any language). Ringu Tulku talked about allowing your mind to be 'unaltered,' 'to be in its most natural state;' 'primordial, natural, original, the way it always was in its true nature.' Here are some more of his actual words, to give further context:

"tam yang ö shu ma chö nyug mä ngang
Then *TAM* also dissolves slowly, from the bottom of the lotus flower upwards, slowly, slowly up until the *nadi*, the dot on the top, and then *ö shu* melts into light.
Then, *ma chö nyug mä ngang* you allow your mind
'unaltered' *ma chö*
nyug mä is 'the way it always was, its true nature'

rang bab so mä long du nyam par shag
rang bab means 'uncontrolled, uncontrived'
rang is 'self' and *bab* means 'the way it settles naturally;' therefore, *rang bab*

so *mä* is 'fresh' or 'freshly'
long du means 'in the space,' or 'in the atmosphere'
nyam par shag means 'meditate' or 'let it remain'
nyam means 'laid down' or 'put down'
nyam par means 'equally'
But here, *nyam par shag* is actually 'meditate' or 'let it remain'

These things are very difficult to translate exactly."

ༀ་ཏུ་རེ་ཏུཏྟཱ་རེ་ཏུ་རེ་སྭཱ་ཧཱ།

ACKNOWLEDGEMENTS

With enormous gratitude to Ringu Tulku for giving these teachings, and ceaseless teachings in myriad forms alongside them. Also, with gratitude to Margaret Richardson for sponsoring the production of this book, which made the whole endeavour possible, and which allows all profits from the sale of this volume to go to further the work of Rigul Trust in Rigul, Ringu Tulku's homeland.

Thank you to Anna Howard for careful proof-reading of the final drafts and for suggestions for the title. Thank you to Paul O'Connor for designing the presentation of the book and Rachel Moffitt for overseeing the administrative side of things. Thank you to those who contributed to the English translation of Tenga Rinpoche's sadhana, including Adam Pearcey for his experienced advice in finalising it. Thank you to the organisers of the original teachings that form the basis of this book. And thank you to the White Tara Meditation Group, in Oxford and further afield, for sharing this practice and general comradeship on the path.

I'd also like to acknowledge the many people in our own day-to-day lives that hold the qualities of White Tara, who inspire us and connect us back to love and peace, healing and harmony, whenever that is needed. Ultimately it may be our own job to do this, but for now I am grateful for the kindness and wisdom of those who have helped me in this way. They include my daughters, Lara and Katie; my grandmother, Phyllis Crawshaw; my long-standing friend, Jane Seymour; and many other wise women I seek counsel from regularly.

May we all find wisdom and healing and peace through these teachings. And may the people of Rigul be supported and sustained, in wisdom and peace, and in health, through funds raised by this volume.

Mary Dechen Jinpa
For Bodhicharya Publications

A note from the founder of Rigul Trust

It has been a privilege for me, as founder of Rigul Trust, to be able to sponsor this White Tara book in loving memory of my late sister and my parents. 100% of profits from the sale of this book will go to benefit Rigul directly, now and in the future, through Rigul Trust; to help fund:

- The school, including free education, free school meals, free boarding, free textbooks, and the teachers' and cooks' salaries.
- The health clinic, including the doctor's and nurse's salary, and the running costs of the clinic for the year.
- The Shedra, including Khenpo's salary and the cost of food for the monks.

Rigul, Tibet is Ringu Tulku's homeland where he has his monastery. The people of Rigul wish to extend their heartfelt gratitude and appreciation to all who have supported them financially, in prayer, in kind and in deed; from every walk of life and from all over the world.

A lovely thought: The money you have paid for this book will help to support the people in Rigul with health, education and poverty relief. A win, win situation.

Wishing all who read this good health, a joyful mind and may your wishes be fulfilled soon. Thank you so much.

Margaret Richardson
Founder of Rigul Trust

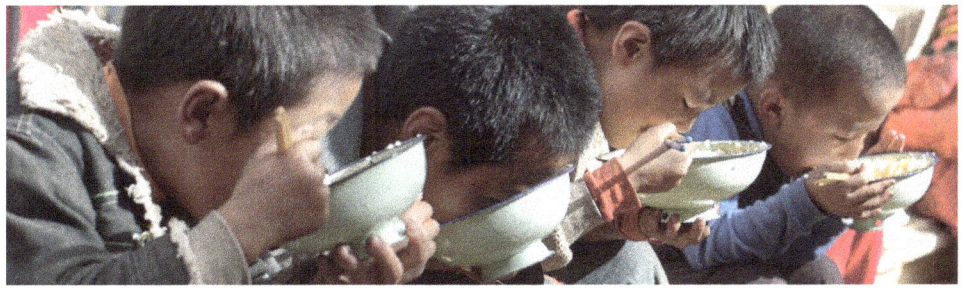

Rigul Trust is a UK Charity whose main aim is to provide funds for the provision of basic health care, education and poverty relief amongst Tibetan refugee communities in India, and in particular for the people of some of the most remote areas of Tibet, such as Rigul.

In Rigul, we currently fund:
The school, including free school meals and the teachers' and cooks' salaries.
The health clinic, funding the doctor, the nurse and the running costs of the clinic.
The shedra, funding the Khenpo and food for the monks.

To find out more, or to make a donation, please visit:

www.rigultrust.org
info@rigultrust.org & donations@rigultrust

Patron: Ringu Tulku Rinpoche - Founder: Margaret Richardson   - UK Charity Registration No: 1124076

About the Author

Ringu Tulku Rinpoche is a Tibetan Buddhist Master of the Kagyu Order. He was trained in all schools of Tibetan Buddhism under many great masters including HH the 16th Gyalwang Karmapa and HH Dilgo Khyentse Rinpoche. He took his formal education at Namgyal Institute of Tibetology, Sikkim and Sampurnananda Sanskrit University, Varanasi, India. He served as Tibetan Textbook Writer and Professor of Tibetan Studies in Sikkim for 25 years.

Since 1990, he has been travelling and teaching Buddhism and meditation in Europe, America, Canada, Australia and Asia. He participates in various interfaith and 'Science and Buddhism' dialogues and is the author of several books on Buddhist topics. These include *Path to Buddhahood, Daring Steps, The Ri-me Philosophy of Jamgon Kongtrul the Great, Confusion Arises as Wisdom*, the *Lazy Lama* series and the *Heart Wisdom* series, as well as several children's books, available in Tibetan and European languages.

He founded the organisations Bodhicharya - see www.bodhicharya.org and Rigul Trust - see www.rigultrust.org.

For an up to date list of books by Ringu Tulku, please visit
www.bodhicharya.org/bookshop

The work and professional skills required to produce this book have been given, partially free of charge and partially kindly sponsored. As a result, all profits from the sale of this book will go to funding projects undertaken by Rigul Trust, which include supporting a school, a health clinic and a shedra for monastic learning, in the Rigul area of Tibet, where Ringu Tulku is originally from.

May there be great benefit and happiness.

www.ingramcontent.com/pod-product-compliance
Lightning Source LLC
Chambersburg PA
CBHW051331110526
44590CB00032B/4476